In Search of
That Which Was Lost

True Symbolism of the Royal Arch

In Search of That Which Was Lost

True Symbolism of the Royal Arch

Duncan Moore

First published 2013

ISBN 978 0 85318 424 9

Published by Lewis Masonic

an imprint of Ian Allan Publishing Ltd, Hersham, Surrey KT12 4RG.
Printed in England.

Visit the Lewis Masonic website at www.lewismasonic.co.uk

Distributed in the United States of America and Canada by BookMasters
Distribution Services.

Front cover:
John Harris miniature Royal Arch Tracing Board. Copyright, and permission of The Library and Museum of Freemasonry, London

All uncredited photographs were taken by the author.

Contents

Published in memory of Duncan Moore

D uncan Moore was born in London and grew up in Lancashire, being educated at Merchant Taylors' School, Crosby and, much later, at the University of Kingston-upon-Thames. He was bitten by the history bug at an early age and was a lifelong student of that subject.

Initiated into Freemasonry in Cheshire in 1971, he held Grand Rank or equivalent in most Masonic Orders. He was involved in various degrees in several English Provinces. He was also a member of the Knight Masons of Ireland and was active in Scotland and Belgium during his lifetime. His particular delight was to witness the *Duncan Moore* expansion of Masonry in the English District of Cyprus, where he was a founder of Mark and RAM lodges and three Rose Croix Chapters.

Duncan Moore was a keen member of the Merseyside and Manchester Associations for Masonic Research and gave many papers to lodges and associations in the north of England and in Cyprus. Having written many histories of Craft Lodges and other Orders, he demonstrated the unique ability to look behind the minutes, to the events on the local and world stage that will have affected the members and conditioned their Masonic membership.

In tackling the subject of symbolism in his previous book *A Guide to Masonic Symbolism*, he was careful to avoid the fantastic and stuck to interpretations of Masonic symbols that are generally acceptable and historically valid. He adopted the same criteria in the present volume.

He will be greatly missed by his wife, Cathy, and a large extended family.

Preface

It has for some time been considered important to refocus the attention of English Freemasons on the importance of the Royal Arch Degree (for such we now admit it is) and thereby to try to raise its profile.

Many brethren go through their Masonic careers paying only lip-service to their membership of their Royal Arch Chapters and indeed some never even join it.

I was exalted into Royal Arch Masonry in September 1977 in Excelsior Engineers Chapter No.4248 (now alas no more). Since that autumnal afternoon in Birkenhead, Cheshire, there have been many changes to the way we do Royal Arch but it is still important to look at what it meant to Companions in the past and also what it means now. As I pointed out in my previous book *A Guide to Masonic Symbolism* a lot of changes wrought particularly at the time of the union of the two Grand Lodges in 1813 resulted in the loss of symbols which nonetheless had great relevance to the meaning of the Degrees of the Craft, the Royal Arch and other things.

It is now, in my view, time for a reappraisal of the Royal Arch and a fresh look at where it sits in the Masonic 'big picture'. That is what this book attempts to provide.

The ritual quotations in this book are largely taken from the Complete Workings (either the current version dated 2008, or from earlier versions), because that was what I grew up with. That said, I have also drawn extensively on rituals from all over the world in order to clarify as much as possible of the symbolism of the Holy Royal Arch.

We begin by looking at the crucial importance of the Royal Arch within the Masonic ethos and then go on briefly to look at the historical background.

Next, we proceed to examine the symbolism of the items of equipment in a Chapter and the function of the officers. The ceremonies of Exaltation, Installation of the Principals and the (in most of England now obsolete) ceremony of Passing the Veils are discussed. Finally we look at how the Royal Arch is practised in other parts of the world.

As the title of this work proclaims, we are in search of 'that which was lost'. I hope reading the following pages will help you to find it and understand it.

Duncan Moore
Larnaca, Cyprus 2013

Acknowledgements

M y sincere thanks are due to Nick Grant, Pip and Martin Faulks and others at Lewis Masonic for their courtesy and assistance during the preparation and publication of this book. I am indebted to the District Grand Lodge and Chapter of Cyprus for allowing me to take a sabbatical from all but essential duties whilst I completed it.

I am also profoundly grateful to Mrs Joan Greenwood for allowing me access to the Royal Arch books and papers of the late Excellent Companion James Paterson Greenwood PAGSoj, Past 2nd Provincial Grand Principal, Yorkshire (West Riding). Jim was much revered in West Yorkshire and also here in Cyprus, where he spent his last few years. The Masonic Centre in Paralimni now bears his name.

I owe particular thanks to two Chapters in Cyprus: St.Paul's Chapter No.2277 and Othello Chapter No.5670 for granting permission to photograph regalia and equipment. I was also obliged to Ex.Comp Arend van Duyvenbode Prov.Asst.G.Scribe E of the Province of West Lancashire for photographs of the beautiful and unusual Egyptian Room in Liverpool Masonic Hall.

The Chapter of Sincerity No.600 in the Province of Yorkshire (West Riding) supplied photographs of the unusual regalia worn by their Principals, for which I was very thankful. Companion Adrian Berry of Othello Chapter was also very helpful with photographs and illustrations.

The Supreme Grand Chapter of Ireland was extremely courteous and helpful, and I owe especial thanks to Rebecca Hayes.

The Bibliography lists the many works I have consulted and my thanks go to their authors, living and dead. I make no apology for repeating John Hamill's words about one of his books: 'I have milked a hundred cows, but the cheese is mine'!

The greatest acknowledgement I must make is to all those Companions who developed and redeveloped the Royal Arch Degree in the first place. I thought I knew a bit about Chapter Masonry, having been a member of the Royal Arch for 35 years, but writing this book has shown me just how much there is to our wonderful Order and how worthy it is of further research, which I hope to some small extent to have stimulated.

My wife Cathy has, in this as in everything else, been a constant source of support and encouragement.

Introduction

To write a book on the Holy Royal Arch degree is to tread in the footsteps of many distinguished scholars who have tried, not unsuccessfully, to unravel its mysteries for nearly three hundred years.

Historians generally acknowledge that all history has to be revisited from time to time in an attempt to bring it up to date in the light of modern knowledge. When I studied history at school, we were taught that King George lll had been insane and that was the end of it. Today, in spite of the sensation caused by the film *The Madness of King George*, many think that he may have been suffering from porphyria, anthrax or some other condition which displayed the symptoms of madness. In my youth there was endless speculation about whether Adolf Hitler had actually died in 1945, or escaped from Europe to South America. Now we know that he was suffering from Parkinson's disease and, although he was only 56, might not have lasted much longer anyway.

In Freemasonry, this consideration is equally applicable. We are, for instance, still finding out things about the Freemasonry which existed prior to the establishment of the Premier Grand Lodge in 1717. The excellent work done by Bro Rev Neville Barker Cryer and others on the Restoration Lodge in Chester is a good example.

The origins of the Royal Arch, like those of the Craft, cannot be pinpointed. Just as we know that the Premier Grand Lodge came into existence in 1717 because four old lodges and some old Masons came together to 'revive' (note that word) an annual grand feast, so we know that the Royal Arch already existed before the first mention of it in Ireland in 1743 when there is a report of the Royal Arch being carried in procession at Youghal, Co. Cork.

Something must have existed before those two dates, but what and in what form? Short of a sudden discovery of a vault full of documents somewhere, we will be forced to rely on snippets of information for all eternity.

One of the purposes of writing this book is to persuade Companions to encourage Master Masons to join the Royal Arch and to try to explain its significance to those who already have joined. Far too often we hear the complaint 'I'm not really into Chapter.' That is partly because it is very different from the Craft in its structure, ritual and everything else – or it appears to be. Many brethren take to the Mark Degree more readily and that is, in part at least, because the structure of a Mark Lodge is far more recognisable to a Craft Mason. What I hope to show here is that the importance and centrality of Royal Arch Masonry make an understanding of it crucial to our Masonic membership. It is true, as the Chinese proverb goes: *'A rising tide does not lift every boat'* but there are many people who could 'get into' Royal Arch if they just took the trouble to observe it and try to understand what it means.

The Royal Arch, as we now have it, is very much about the history of the Jewish race from the Tabernacle in the wilderness, via King Solomon's Temple to the rebuilding of that Temple under Zerubbabel, Haggai and Joshua or Jeshua. The central theme of the Degree is a search for something lost and that is the true name of God. This concept, however, did not start with the Jews. The ancient Egyptian Sun God, Ra, when on earth, was bitten by a serpent and this resulted in great pain. He entreated his daughter, Isis, to use her healing powers to get rid of the pain but she refused unless he would reveal his true name. After refusing to do so twice Ra finally capitulated, and Isis was later revered because she was in possession of this secret.[1]

There is also the story of Enoch, the fifth from Seth and the seventh from Adam. From Genesis (5:24) we learn that his life was one of exceptional virtue; he is described as *'walking with God.'* He is said to have lived 365 years, his earthly life ending not by death but by being bodily transported to Heaven (Genesis 5:23). We are told he received the gift of wisdom and knowledge from God and was learned in astronomy and astrology. Tradition tells us that God, seeing in Enoch a man of perfect virtue, elected to reveal to him His true name.

After receiving that name in a dream, Enoch's vision continued and he was conveyed through nine arches into a subterranean vault which contained a triangular plate of gold upon which was written the name of God. Enoch took the dream as a sign from God and after a long journey through the Holy Land, he excavated nine apartments vertically into the earth each covered with an arch, the lowest of which was hewn out of solid rock. In this apartment he placed an alabaster pedestal and mounted upon it a cube of agate into one side of which he had sunk a triangular plate of gold inscribed with the name of the Deity – thus fulfilling the purpose of his vision.

Above the apartments he built a modest temple of unhewn stones with a secret passage into the apartments under a stone with a ring through it. Enoch was worshipped in Ancient Egypt and among Moslems as Idris. It is thought that Enoch's temple was located on Mount Moriah in Jerusalem,

---

1 *Side Lights on the Holy Royal Arch* by F.G.Harmer

the site Abraham's sacrifice and of King Solomon's, Zerubbabel's and King Herod's Temples.

The ritual of the Royal Order of Scotland tells us that Enoch created two pillars, one of brick and the other of stone and engraved all the knowledge of the world on both of them so that if the pillar of brick was destroyed by water, the pillar of stone would remain and if the stone pillar should be destroyed by fire there would still be the pillar of brick.

The Royal Arch of Enoch.

The pillar of brick was destroyed by water (Noah's flood) and the stone pillar survived which the Jewish historian, Josephus, claimed could be seen in his day (shortly after Christ) in the land of Siriad. These I believe were what the two great pillars of King Solomon's Temple were based on, the idea, communicated to us in the Second Degree Tracing Board, that they were a repository for the constitutional rolls having been described by at least one Masonic scholar as ridiculous.[2]

Enoch's dream and his subsequent actions sound like an earlier version of our own Royal Arch legend and are the subject of the degree of Royal Arch of Enoch in the Ancient and Accepted Scottish Rite, or Rose Croix, where it derived from Etienne Morin's Rite of 25 Degrees, preserved in the Francken Manuscript of 1783, a copy of which is held in our Grand Lodge (see Appendix 2). That said, it would appear that all versions of the Royal Arch have a unifying underlying theme of a quest for the True Name of God.[3]

The Book of Exodus, in chapter 36, tells us how the First or Holy Lodge came into being in around 1446 BC. After God had given the Ten Commandments, He called Moses up into the mountain, where he remained forty days and forty nights. During that time, God told him to speak to the Israelites, asking them to give gold, silver, brass, blue, purple, fine linen, oil, precious stones, and other things, to make a tabernacle or

2   *A Guide to Masonic Symbolism* by Duncan Moore
3   *The Mystery of the Royal Arch Word* by Arturo de Hoyos – Pietre–Stones Review of Freemasonry

sanctuary, where God would dwell among them. Here we see the origin of the veils of the tabernacle and also the holy vessels.

God showed Moses the pattern of this tabernacle, with its coverings, its holy place and most holy place, its ark of the covenant with the two cherubim and mercy-seat, its table for the shewbread, golden candlestick, and altar of incense, and the garments for Aaron and his sons. Everything was accurately described by God. Then God instructed Moses as to who could do the work He had commanded to be done, and named two to whom He had given special wisdom and skill. These two were Bezaleel and Aholiab.

When Moses came down from the mountain he called Aaron and all the people of Israel, and told them what God had commanded. The people willingly brought gifts, until more than enough was provided. Then Bezaleel and Aboliab, and other 'wise-hearted men', worked diligently until the tabernacle and all things belonging to it were made exactly as God had instructed. Some worked in gold and silver, others in brass and wood; wise women spun cloth of blue, purple and scarlet, and fine linen; precious stones were set for the high priest's – ephod and breastplate; and, at last, all was finished. Then we are told in Exodus, '*Moses did look upon all the work, and, behold, they had done it as the Lord had commanded.*' Then Moses blessed them.

The tabernacle then accompanied the Israelites in their wanderings through the wilderness.

Much later, after King David had unified Israel and bought land from Araunah the Jebusite for the purpose of providing a permanent House of God, the first temple was constructed by David's son, Solomon, with the help of men and materials supplied by Hiram, King of Tyre and the curious and masterly workmanship of another Tyrian, Hiram Abif. This was the Second or Sacred Lodge.

Now presumably these people did know the sacred Name of God but did not dare to pronounce it and substituted the word Adonai, which is still in use in Jewish prayers and of course we have the Masonic motto '*Kodesh l'Adonai*' – Holiness to the Lord. Even within our Royal Arch ceremonies the genuine Word is only used in restricted circumstances, as our obligation directs us. As we will see there were at one time two words in the Royal Arch and the same care was used. We refer to God as The True and Living God Most High for most of the ceremony. To the Jews the sacred name was called the shem hameforash – the unspoken name of God. Within our Degree we have other names for God – El Shaddai, El Elohim, etc. The genuine Word is written only in consonants YHVH because that is how Hebrew was written and so we have no idea how it was pronounced. Usually, in the Bible, God is referred to as the LORD (*sic* in capitals) but some modern versions refer to Him as Yahweh which is Hebrew for 'He is' and so accords with the name God used to describe Himself when He appeared to Moses out of the burning bush – I AM.

Then we have the Third or Grand and Royal Lodge founded by Zerubbabel, Prince of the people, Haggai the prophet and Joshua, the son of Josedech, the high priest. Please note where I have placed the commas – it was Joshua himself and not his father who was the high priest. We will look at who these people were when we consider the functions of the Principals who represent them in a Royal Arch Chapter (see chapter 4) but for now let us be content with the legend attached to them. They were real people and they did facilitate the rebuilding of the Temple, although the rest of our story is a legend allowing us to regain that which is lost in the Third Degree. Considering the real facts, this whole thing happened because Cyrus, King of Persia, having conquered Babylon decided to let the Israelites return to their native land and to rebuild their Temple. Without this none of the true facts of this period would have occurred and we say in our ceremony that Cyrus was inspired by God to take this action.

We will look at these Three Grand Lodges in more detail in Chapter 5 when we come to examine how the Royal Arch got to us.

CHAPTER 1

Why is the Royal Arch Important?

The Second Article of the Union of the two Grand Lodges in 1813 states that: *Pure and ancient Masonry consists of three degrees and three degrees only: those of Entered Apprentice, Fellowcraft and Master Mason including the Supreme Order of the Holy Royal Arch.*

This statement requires some amplification because what it is saying is that the Royal Arch is not a degree per se, but merely a part of a degree. Until just a few years ago we used to tell our candidates:

'You may perhaps imagine that you have this day received a fourth degree in Masonry. Such however is not the case; it is the Master Mason's Degree completed.'

Now this always puzzled me. We meet separately from the Craft lodge, we go on a different night, we wear different regalia, we call ourselves Companion, instead of Brother, our warrant is called a Charter and our meetings are called Convocations. How, then, can it not be a separate degree?

The answer is that, yes, it is a separate degree in terms of regalia, titles, etc. It was practised as a separate degree at one time, as we shall see in the next chapter. In this sense the Installation of a Master in the Craft is a degree as well, in that it is a conferment of Masonic knowledge to those who are qualified to receive it in the form of specific secret signs, tokens and words. This is perhaps a useful definition of what a 'degree' is and the same set of criteria could be equally applied to the installation into the three chairs of the Royal Arch. Looking at it from that point of view there are eight degrees in 'pure and ancient masonry': Entered Apprentice, Fellowcraft, Master Mason, Installation (which has not had to happen before Exaltation since 1835 – see next chapter), Exaltation in a Royal Arch Chapter and then Installation as Third Principal Joshua, Second Principal Haggai and First Principal Zerubbabel.

But the ceremony of Exaltation remains part of the Craft Mason's Third Degree because that is what it was intended for in the first place. If we are no longer to use the word 'completion' we still have to understand just where the Royal Arch fits in and that by fitting in where it does it is crucial to the whole Masonic experience.

The Supreme Grand Chapter website uses the words 'the culmination of pure and ancient masonry'. It goes on to say:

The Craft gives its members eminently practical rules by which they can live their lives in the service of both God, however they worship Him, and the community as a whole.

Man, however, is not simply a practical being but has an essential spiritual aspect to his nature. This is taken up in the Royal Arch, in which the candidate, without trespassing on the bounds of religion, is led to contemplate the nature of God and his personal relationship with Him.

Thus the Royal Arch leads the candidate from the practical to the spiritual and completes 'pure ancient masonry', a fascinating journey of self-knowledge and self-discovery beginning with the Entered Apprentice degree and culminating in the First Principal's chair of the Chapter.[4]

So it seems a pity that so many Masons only got half the story. They were informed, when they were raised to the Third Degree, that there is more. They learnt that all you've got now is *substituted* secrets and that they must join the Holy Royal Arch to find the genuine ones. Some don't bother – my own grandfathers never did. But I think pure curiosity would have overcome me long ago if I knew there was something else there but I didn't know what it was. I didn't join the Royal Arch from curiosity. I joined because I had taken up my Masonic career in earnest and I knew that joining the Chapter was the next logical step.

The crux of the matter, though, surely lies in what we've just looked at from the Supreme Grand Chapter website: *'to contemplate the nature of God and his personal relationship with Him'*. What that means is that, in the Craft, we are taught practical lessons. We start with a rough ashlar in the First Degree which, by means of contemplation and the symbolism inherent in that degree, we convert into a perfect ashlar in the Second Degree, in which we are exhorted to study nature and science. As we will see in the next chapter, that used to be as far as it went. Then the Third Degree came along to encourage us to consider the after-life in terms of facing death with equanimity. But it also contains a legendary history in which secrets are lost, substituted and left to be found somewhere else.

And that 'somewhere else' is in a Royal Arch Chapter, which emphasises our total dependence on God and describes the Royal Arch Degree as *'at once the foundation and keystone of the whole Masonic structure'*. This is why the Supreme Order of the Holy Royal Arch is a crucial, essential and fundamental part of Masonry which no serious student of our Masonic Craft can possibly afford to ignore.

To put it another way: the Royal Arch is the key which unlocks the mysteries of the Craft Degrees.

The late Lt.-Cdr. C. R. Manasseh put it like this:

There is, in my opinion, a very good reason for separating the three Craft or blue degrees from the Royal Arch ceremony; for the blue degrees take us through our experiences during our life on this earth and the Royal Arch then tries to initiate us into the Grand

---

4   Supreme Grand Chapter of England website

Mystery of the Life hereafter. And just as death on earth is not the final end of Man's saga, so the Third degree in the 'Blue' is not the end of our Masonic teaching. In fact, this is implied when the candidate is 'raised from a figurative death' but is left wondering in the Limbo of Unknowing, when he is told that 'the genuine secrets of a master mason were lost by the untimely death of our Master H.A.'. To tide him over, however, the candidate is given certain 'substituted secrets', a sort of Ariadne's thread or guide through the maze which mystically points out the timeless transition between life on earth and life hereafter. We find this same teaching in Greek mythology and mysteries (Eleusinian), as well as in almost every other mystical writings (the Cloud of Unknowing, the Dark Night of St. John of the Cross, etc.).

Now, if the Royal Arch were not an integral part of Craft Masonry, the latter would be an incomplete teaching. In fact, it would no longer be mystical but purely allegorical, because the essence of a mystical teaching is to give man a glimpse of what lies beyond death and to show him its intimate connection with what lies this side of death: birth and life are otherwise as inexplicable as death.[5]

In the Third Degree we learn that we are moving from the east to the west *in search of that which was lost.* In the First Degree we were concerned with the needs of the body, the body that has now left the profane world in search of light. In the Second Degree we concentrate on the soul by contemplating the intellectual faculty. But in the Third Degree we are concerned with the spirit. As man consists of body, soul and spirit, so King Solomon's Temple was a tripartite structure, consisting of a Porch, an Inner (or Middle) Chamber and the Holy of Holies. We go west then in search of the True Name of God. We head in that direction although we don't actually get to the west because that means death, and of course we don't in the Third Degree actually find what we're looking for but return only with substituted secrets. Death will eventually overtake all of us but in the meantime we have undergone a symbolical, figurative death in the Third Degree and have been raised to a figurative new life. Now we have to complete the process by increasing our knowledge of God.

---

5   Lt.-Cdr. C. R. Manasseh – *The Mysticism of the Royal Arch*

CHAPTER 2

How did the Royal Arch get to us?

The precious treasure, long concealed,
Was by three worthy knights revealed,
Where erst a temple stood.

Its ancient ruins they explored,
And found the Grand Mysterious Word,
Made known before the flood.[6]

Biblical Legends

We hear in the after-dinner colloquy between the First Principal and the Principal Sojourner that there were three original Grand Lodges. These were not of course lodges because there were no lodges in those days. What the words refer to is three points in history at which God commanded the Children of Israel to build Him a place of worship.

The First or Holy 'Lodge' was established two years after Moses led the Israelites out of Egypt. They crossed the Red Sea (or the Reed Sea – see chapter 10) and pitched their tents at the foot of Mount Horeb in the Wilderness of Sinai. We learn that God had already dictated the Ten Commandments.

We all know who Moses was but what of Aholiab and Bezaleel who collaborated with him in erecting the First or Holy Lodge? In Exodus chapter 31 it says:

Then the LORD spoke to Moses, saying: 'See, I have called by name Bezaleel the son of Uri, the son of Hur, of the tribe of Judah. And I have filled him with the Spirit of God, in wisdom, in understanding, in knowledge, and in all manner of workmanship, to design artistic works, to work in gold, in silver, in bronze, in cutting jewels for setting, in carving wood, and to work in all manner of workmanship. And I, indeed I, have appointed with him Aholiab the son of Ahisamach, of the tribe of Dan; and I have put wisdom in the hearts of all who are gifted artisans, that they may make all that I have commanded you.

This description of Bezaleel's talents is similar to the description of Hiram Abif in Second Chronicles chapter 2.

Exodus 31 goes on to say: *The tabernacle of meeting, the ark of the Testimony and the mercy seat that is on it, and all the furniture of the tabernacle; the table and its*

---

6   *The Mystery of the Royal Arch Word* by Arturo de Hoyos – Pietre–Stones Review of
Freemasonry

utensils, the pure gold lampstand with all its utensils, the altar of incense, the altar of burnt offering with all its utensils, and the laver and its base; the garments of ministry, the holy garments for Aaron the priest and the garments of his sons, to minister as priests, and the anointing oil and sweet incense for the holy place. According to all that I have commanded you they shall do.

Then we come to the Second or Sacred Lodge, founded by Solomon, King of Israel, Hiram, King of Tyre and Hiram Abif, the widow's son. This came about because Israel, having had leaders like Moses and Joshua (of the extended day), who were leaders but not kings had gone through a period when the land was ruled by Judges. Eventually (as we shall see in discussing the Installation scripture readings) the prophet Samuel chose Saul as the first king of Israel, but Saul failed the tests that God set him and he then chose David. David bought the land on which the Temple would be built and drew up the plans but the actual building was left to his son, Solomon.

So this was King Solomon's Temple in which was rehoused in the Most Holy Place the Ark of the Covenant which is described graphically in the ritual of the Degree of Royal Master in the Cryptic rite as follows:

It was a small chest or coffer, 2 cubits and a half in length and a cubit and a half in width and depth. It was made of wood, excepting only the mercy seat, and overlaid with gold both inside and out. It had a ledge of gold surrounding it at the top, into which was let the cover called the mercy seat. The mercy seat was of solid gold, the thickness of a hand's breadth; at the ends were two Cherubim looking inwards towards each other with their wings expanded which, embracing the whole circumference of the mercy seat, met in the middle on each side. All the Rabbis say it was made out of the same mass without any soldering of parts. Here the Shekinah or Divine Presence rested and was visible in the appearance of a cloud over it. Hence the Bath-Kol issued and gave answers when God was consulted.

Here it was that God was said in the Scriptures to dwell between the Cherubim, that is between the Cherubim on the mercy seat, because there was the seat or throne of the visible presence of His glory amongst them.[7]

What we should note here is the ledge or plate of gold, because it is on a plate of gold that our Sojourners find the Word.[8]

But we learn something else as well. When the three Grand Masters deposited replicas of the Ark and all its contents in the ninth arch of the sacred vault beneath the Holy of Holies, the Master Word, which is the object of our Royal Arch search, was deposited on top of the Ark in three

---

7   The Lecture in the Degree of Royal Master, Ceremonies of the Order of Royal and Select Masters
8   *The Mystery of the Royal Arch Word* by Arturo de Hoyos – Pietre–Stones Review of Freemasonry

languages – Chaldean, Syrian and Egyptian – so that if the Israelites were ever taken into captivity and forgot their mother tongue, when it was found again it might be interpreted by means of the other languages. But there is more: they also placed the jewels (or signets) of the three Grand Masters on top of the Ark inscribed in these languages *'knowing that the descriptions thereof would be handed down to the latest posterity'*.

We should also bear in mind that in both the Tabernacle in the wilderness and in King Solomon's Temple, God was physically present.

Now we know the story from the Craft. The genuine secrets were lost at the death of Hiram Abif and so we have a Third or Grand and Royal Lodge under Zerubbabel, Haggai and Joshua, the son of Josedech, the High Priest. The Irish legend is a different one and concerns the repair of the Temple under King Josiah (see Chapter 12 on Irish Royal Arch Masonry). As we have seen, the Third or Grand and Royal Lodge, which is the *raison d'être* behind our Degree, only happened because Cyrus, King of Persia let the Israelites return to their native land. Why he did this is a matter for debate but basically he was intelligent enough to avoid repeating the mistakes of the Babylonian kings who had preceded him. Don't forget Cyrus was a Persian who had conquered Babylon after the death of Nebuchadnezzar and following the prophecy at Belshazzar's feast when Nebuchadnezzar's regent and successor unashamedly used goblets looted from King Solomon's Temple. God's words then appeared on the wall: *'Mene, Mene, tekel upharsin'*, roughly translated as 'You have been tried in the balances and found wanting and your land will be divided and given to the Medes and Persians'. So for the Babylonian dynasty the writing was quite literally on the wall.

The lesson Cyrus, when he took over, had to learn from previous mistakes was quite simply that the Babylonian kings had invaded and conquered other countries and brought the people captive to Babylon, where they enslaved them and they then became a liability. He determined that those people would be better off back in their own countries where they could do useful work and provide him with a line of defence against his old enemy – Egypt. Whether he was inspired by God to do this we will never know but the Jews thought so because it was fulfilling their prophecies that they would return some day and rebuild their Temple, which to Cyrus was useful work for them to do. The decree Cyrus issued was as follows:

Cyrus, The King, to Sysina and Sarabason, sendeth greeting.
Be it known unto you, that I have given leave to all the Jews that are in my dominions, to return into their own Country, and there to rebuild their Capital City, with the Holy Temple at Jerusalem, in the same place where it stood before. I have likewise sent

my messenger, Mithridates and Zerubbabel, the Governor of Judea, to superintend the building, and to see it raised sixty cubits upward from the ground and as many over; the walls to be three rows of polished stones, and one of the wood of the Country, together with an Altar for Sacrifices; and all this to be done at my charge.

It is my further pleasure that they receive entire to themselves, all the profits and revenues that were formerly enjoyed by their predecessors, and that they have an allowance paid them of 205,500 drachmas, in consideration of beasts for Sacrifices, wine and oil; and 2,500 measures of wheat, in lieu of fine flour, and all this to be raised upon the tribute of Samaria; that the priests may offer up sacrifices according to the laws and ceremonies of Moses, and pray daily for the King and the Royal family, and for the welfare and happiness of the Persian Empire: and let no man presume to do anything contrary to the tenor of this my royal will and proclamation, upon pain of forfeiting life and estate.

CYRUS.

One of Cyrus' decrees of tolerance (because this wasn't the only one) won him the soubriquet 'Father of Human Rights' and a copy of that decree which was found in a cylinder stands at the entrance to the United Nations in New York.[9]

Not all of the Israelites wanted to return. Many of them had set up successful businesses in Babylon which they were not willing to abandon in a hurry. Those who returned were not welcome in some quarters. But return they did and Cyrus gave them documents to allow them to do so, as well as the holy vessels from King Solomon's Temple that Nebuchadnezzar had filched seventy years before. To go back to Nebuchadnezzar; he was a Chaldean (Abraham's birth place is known as Ur of the Chaldes). These Chaldeans had taken over from the Assyrians after the latter had invaded the northern part of Palestine, in which lived Israelites and Samaritans. They had taken many captives and brought them to Babylon. The southern part of the country – Judea – was not affected by this and Jerusalem and its temple, with all that meant to the Jews, continued intact.

So, at first, as the ritual tells us when Nebuchadnezzar sent his general, Nebuzaradan, to bring Judea to heel as well, the only things (apart from King Jehoiachin[10] and his people) to disappear were the holy vessels we've

---

9   Simon Sebag Montefiore – *Jerusalem: the Biography.*
10 Jehoiachin should not be confused with Jehoakim, who had been Nebuchadnezzar's vassal for three years when he offended both Nebuchadnezzar and God by his wickedness: *Surely these things happened to Judah according to the Lord's command, in order to remove them from his presence because of the sins of Manasseh and all he had done, including the shedding of innocent blood. For he had filled Jerusalem with innocent blood, and the Lord was not willing to forgive.* (1 Kings 24:1). Jehoiakim died and Jehoiachin (who was his son) succeeded. That was when the first invasion and 'carrying off' took place.

just been talking about. The Temple was again left intact and a puppet king called Mattaniah was placed on the throne. To emphasise the fact that Nebuchadnezzar expected compliance from Mattaniah, the latter's name was changed to Zedekiah which (somewhat ironically) means the 'Justice of YHVH' to remind him of what was in store for him if he failed to toe the party line. Mattaniah/Zedekiah was a disreputable character and broke his promises so the army of the Chaldeans again invaded. Zedekiah tried to escape but was caught, blinded and bound in fetters of brass, fulfilling the prophecy that the last King of Judah would be carried to Babylon, but his eyes would not see it, though he would die there. This escaping party are what is meant by *'those who fled when the city and holy temple were oppressed'*.

A decent fellow called Gedeliah was appointed Governor of Judea but was assassinated soon afterwards. It was then that the remnant of the people were carried to Babylon, leaving behind only the menial tribe who tilled the land – who are described in the Second Book of Kings as not a tribe but just some poor agricultural folk.

Sheshbazzar was appointed by Cyrus as the first Governor of Judea. There is some argument as to whether he and Zerubbabel were one and the same person. From the wording of Cyrus' decree above it would appear so.

So when the Jews did return why weren't they welcome? In the intervening seventy years or so, the remaining Jews and the Samaritans who lived around Jerusalem had practised Judaism as they understood it. But the religion had developed in Babylon and the returning exiles looked on these 'natives' as half-heathen, referring to them as *Am Ha-Aretz* (people of the land – the menial tribe again). Tensions arose and for about three years the rebuilding was suspended. Cyrus died in battle at quite a young age and Darius eventually succeeded. Zerubbabel appealed to him to let the work on the temple recommence, to which Darius acceded. This was in about 518 BC and it is the last we hear of Zerubbabel. We will read more about him in Chapter 5, as we will of Nehemiah who didn't come to Jerusalem for another fifty years.

Zerubbabel had dedicated the altar at the Temple Mount and hired artisans to proceed with the rebuilding. Many of the Jews saw him as their future king (which is why in our Chapters we accord him a sceptre bearing a crown), anticipating the coming of the Messiah, but he was never more than governor and it is possible that Darius eventually had him executed – perhaps because he saw him as a potential danger.

In 515 BC the Temple was dedicated by its priests and many animals were sacrificed. It was much more modest than the first temple and disappointed many of the Jews. Eventually they lost interest in it and it fell into disrepair. It was repaired under King Josiah (see the Irish legend in Chapter 12) but eventually Herod the Great totally rebuilt it as a 'wonder of the world'.[11]

Our Royal Arch Ceremony

But where did the legend we now practise as part of our Royal Arch ceremony come from? We find two things – a sacred scroll and then the Word itself.

Concentrating on the first discovery – the scroll of the sacred scriptures – it bears a strong resemblance to the events recorded by Philostorgius, a Cappadocian historian who lived from about 368 to 439 AD. This story of Julian the Apostate, and his attempt to again rebuild the temple (albeit from bad motives) will be familiar to members of the Order of the Red Cross of Constantine:

When Julian bade the city of Jerusalem to be rebuilt in order to refute openly the predictions of our Lord concerning it, he brought about exactly the opposite of what he intended. For his work was checked by many other prodigies from heaven; and especially, during the preparation of the foundations, one of the stones which was placed at the lowest part of the base, suddenly started from its place and opened the door of a certain cave hollowed out in the rock. Owing to its depth, it was difficult to see what was within this cave; so persons were appointed to investigate the matter, who, being anxious to find out the truth, let down one of their workmen by means of a rope. On being lowered down he found stagnant water reaching up to his knee; and, having gone round the place and felt the walls on every side, he found the cave to be a perfect square. Then, in his return, as he stood near about the middle, he struck his foot against a column which stood rising

The Al-Aqsa Mosque on the Temple Mount in Jerusalem.

---

11   Simon Sebag Montefiore – *Jerusalem: the Biography.*

slightly above the water. As soon as he touched this pillar, he found lying upon it a book wrapped up in a very fine and thin linen cloth; and as soon as he had lifted it up just as he had found it, he gave a signal to his companions to draw him up again. As soon as he regained the light, he showed them the book, which struck them all with astonishment, especially because it appeared so new and fresh, considering the place where it had been found. This book, which appeared such a mighty prodigy in the eyes of both heathens and Jews, as soon as it was opened showed the following words in large letters: 'In the beginning was the Word, and the Word was with God, and the Word was God.' In fact, the volume contained that entire Gospel which had been declared by the divine tongue of the (beloved) disciple and the Virgin. Moreover, this miracle, together with other signs which were then shown from heaven, most clearly showed that 'the word of the Lord would never go forth void,' which had foretold that the devastation of the Temple should be perpetual. For that book declared Him who had uttered those words long before, to be God and the Creator of the universe; and it was a very clear proof that 'their labour was but lost that built,' seeing that the immutable decree of the Lord had condemned the Temple to eternal desolation. The city of Jerusalem itself was formerly called Jebus, and was inhabited by some of the tribe of Benjamin, before King David took it by the aid of Joab. The army promised him the throne of Israel if he could only get possession of that city, and when he captured it, the army faithfully observed its promises. He then built a new city on the same site, and chose it as the metropolis of the entire Hebrew race.

Ammianus Marcellinus adds this: *Julian thought to rebuild at an extravagant expense the proud Temple once at Jerusalem, and committed this task to Alypius who set vigorously to work, and was seconded by the Roman Governor; when fearful balls of fire, breaking out near the foundations, continued their attacks, till the workmen, after repeated scorchings, could approach no more: and he gave up the attempt.*

So here we have an instance of a loss and finding of the sacred scriptures in circumstances not dissimilar to our Royal Arch Legend. There are other legends with similar content by Nicephorous Callistus in his *Ecclesiastical History* and in *Orbis Miraculum* published in 1659 by Samuel Lee.[12] All of these will have been around by the time our ritual was framed and it is quite possible that other legends were adapted to put together the 'big picture'.

So to get back to the original point, the two discoveries. The first, the scriptures presumably comes from one or all of the stories and legends quoted above. The second – the Sacred Name – is an ancient sacred quest going back to Enoch and the Ancient Egyptians, as we saw in the Introduction to this book. So the framers of our ritual, looking for genuine secrets to supplant the substituted ones, determined to incorporate two ancient mysteries into what has evolved into our present Royal Arch ceremony.

---

12 Bernard E. Jones – *Freemasons' Book of the Royal Arch.*

The Degree in its Earliest Period in England

We are probably all aware of the formation of the Premier Grand Lodge in London on 24 June 1717. That meeting of four old lodges at the Goose and Gridiron Tavern in St. Paul's Churchyard is seen as the key date after which the recorded history of Freemasonry can be checked and researched. We also know that something existed before that because obviously four old lodges (at least) existed and they stated it was their intention to 'revive' the Quarterly Communication and the Grand Feast.

In Anderson's first Constitutions of 1723, the author refers the 'Master's to congregate the members of the lodge into a chapter'. This could mislead us and research has shown that this is a matter of interchangeability of terms common in the early eighteenth century and, as John Hamill says, 'nowhere in the minutes (of lodges in that period) is there any reference which could be conjured by even the wildest of Masonic imaginations into even an oblique reference to the Royal Arch.'[13]

Pick and Knight say that the Royal Arch may have existed 'in embryo' as early as 1725.[14] What they base this on will be made clear shortly.

The third Grand Master of the Premier Grand Lodge was Dr. John Theophilus Desaguliers (1683-1744), a Protestant Huguenot whose family had escaped from La Rochelle in France to avoid the persecution which took place after the revocation of the Edict of Nantes in 1685. There were many Huguenots in London at this time (particularly around Holborn and Spitalfields) because life in Louis XIV's Catholic France had become too 'hot' for them. By profession, Desaguliers was a natural philosopher and engineer. He also became an Anglican priest. His talents were recognised in a number of places. In 1725, he became a Fellow of the Royal Society in which he won the prestigious Copley Medal on several occasions, latterly for his discovery of the properties of electricity. He worked closely with Sir Isaac Newton, popularising the latter's theories and has been credited as the inventor of the planetarium. He also prophesied the splitting of the atom 200 years before it happened.

A very clever man, he is also thought to have been the possible originator of both the Master Mason's Degree and the Holy Royal Arch. It seems that he had knowledge of and practised more than three degrees.[15]

We also know that, within a few years of 1717, Masonry spread to continental Europe and that the first recorded instance of a lodge in France was in 1725. It is known that Scots Masons, followers of the Jacobite cause, after the failure of the Jacobite Rising in England in

---

13 John Hamill – *Anderson's 1723 Constitutions and the Royal Arch* – AQC102 1989
14 *The Freemason's Pocket Reference Book* by F.L.Pick and G.N.Knight
15 *York Mysteries Revealed* by Rev Neville Barker Cryer 2006

1715 served in the French army and associated with – largely aristocratic – Frenchmen who wanted a system which they deemed superior to the ordinary Craft degrees, hence the appellation 'Scottish', or 'Ecossais' and the term 'Higher Degrees'.

In 1732 Loge L'Anglaise (The English Lodge) was formed in Bordeaux (becoming No.2 on the roll of the Grand Lodge of France). Soon the French Grand Lodge started working 'Scottish' degrees, creating the tradition in Bordeaux of the Mother Lodge of the world being in Scotland at Kilwinning.

To briefly exclaim what 'Kilwinning' means in Masonic terms, Lodge Mother Kilwinning is number Zero on the roll of the Grand Lodge of Scotland and can prove existence back to before 1598. Because of various factors which are beyond our scope, Mother Kilwinning at one time issued warrants to new lodges, some as far away as Antigua. So there are now many lodges on the Scottish roll with the suffix 'Kilwinning' after their name, many (but not all) of which received their original warrant or charter from Lodge Mother Kilwinning No.0.

Later in that same year of 1732, interest in Scottish or Higher Degree Masonry spread to England. A 'Scottish' lodge met at the Devil's Tavern in Temple Bar, London.

In 1735 at a special meeting at the Bear Inn in Bath, the Master, Wardens and nine brethren received the Degree of Scottish Master, imported from France. The Lodge in which this happened still exists as Royal Cumberland Lodge No.41. From early French exposures we can discern in the Degree of Scottish Master the beginnings of our Royal Arch Degree, as the following catechism demonstrates:

Q. *Are you a Scottish Master?*

A. *I was brought out of the captivity in Babylon.*

Q. *Who honoured you with the Degree of Ecossais (Scottish)?*

A. *Prince Zerubbabel of the line of David and Solomon.*

Q. *When?*

A. *Seventy years after the destruction of the holy city.*

Q. *In what are Ecossais Masons occupied?*

A. *In rebuilding the Temple of God.*

Q. *Why do the Ecossais Masons carry the sword and buckler?*

A. *In memory of the order given by Nehemiah to all workmen at the time of the rebuilding of the Temple, to have swords always at their sides and their bucklers near at hand, for use in case of attack by their enemies.*

It goes without saying that some of this sounds familiar to us. There are other factors involved but Chevalier Andrew Michael Ramsay's famous oration in 1737, which traced the pedigree of Masonry back to the Crusaders, the Knights Hospitaller and other mediaeval orders of chivalry, also makes reference to the concept of the Royal Arch and uses Royal Arch terms. For example he talks of the apostasy of the Jews and the building of the second Temple where the craftsmen worked with trowel in one hand and sword in the other as in the ritual given above.[16]

Ramsay's oration greatly influenced the future development of Masonry and whilst the earliest Masons – who began by only working two Degrees (or possibly even one) and had only started working the Master Mason degree in the 1730s (although Pick and Knight claim that it could have existed in some form from 1723 or 5)[17] – were content that it should be complete in itself and that the genuine secrets would be found 'beyond the veil of time', others believed that a means of 'repairing that loss' would be a useful addition and from around 1740 onwards we see the Royal Arch being worked in England, Scotland and Ireland.

Chevalier Ramsay was another Fellow of the Royal Society and was also associated with John Theophilus Desaguliers in the Gentlemen's Club of Spalding, a society strongly associated with Freemasonry. In order to strengthen his claim of pedigree back to mediaeval knights and such, Ramsay is thought to have invented a rite of seven degrees called the Rite de Bouillon (or Boulogne) of which the Degree of Scottish Master above is one. The name of that rite come from Godfrey (or Geoffrey) de Bouillon, who led the First Crusade in 1099 which delivered Jerusalem into Christian hands. He later declined to be King of Jerusalem because he refused to wear a crown of gold where his Saviour had worn a crown of thorns and instead accepted the title of 'Defender of the Holy Sepulchre'.

From what you have read, you should have learnt that the Scottish Rite has little or nothing to do with Scotland but is a ritual system begun in France and then exported to the new world, where it is still very much in existence, and throughout Europe. English Masons tend to have difficulty in assimilating this fact and believe that it is the ritual worked in lodges in Scotland. This is not correct.

In England, Scotland and Ireland, the Higher Scottish Rite Degrees referred to are now part of what we call the Ancient and Accepted Rite or Rose Croix. The 15th Degree of Knight of the Sword or of the East and the 16th Prince of Jerusalem in that rite are very similar to the

<hr>

16 Ramsay's Oration – Grand Lodge version
17 *The Freemason's Pocket Reference Book* by F.L.Pick and G.N.Knight (Frederick Muller 1955)

Scottish Master Degree we have just been looking at and, indeed, the Scottish Master, or more correctly now Scottish Master of St. Andrew Degree is still worked as part of the Rectified Scottish Rite in France and Belgium and now in England as one of the Degrees leading to the Order of Knights Beneficent of the Holy City which has now been opened up to English Knights Templar.

Aside from this, in the opinion of many scholars, the Royal Arch comes from a different starting point than the Craft. The Craft is about adapting practical lessons and symbols from the operative craft of the stonemason to the speculative science. It is true to say that the Third Degree is somewhat dramatic but far less so than the Royal Arch which admits to being 'somewhat in dramatic form' and in fact is in part a play with a dramatic narrative between the First Principal and the Principal Sojourner with occasional input from other *dramatis personae*. It is thought that the roots of the Royal Arch lie more in Rosicrucianism and alchemy as well as in Ramsay's aspirations to a knightly pedigree.[18]

Furthermore, as we have already seen in the preceding chapter, whereas the Craft is about our relationship towards each other and the rest of our fellow men, the Royal Arch is about our relationship with God.

Having said all that, what else do we know? The first recorded (i.e. minuted) conferment of the Royal Arch Degree is that of three brethren in Fredericksburg Lodge, Virginia, America, on December 22, 1753. America was then of course still a British colony. This, however, does not really mean much because we have earlier references to the Royal Arch nearer home.

A further indication comes from the records of the Grand Lodge of All England which had headquarters in the city of York. That Grand Lodge existed from around 1705 and it was gone by the end of the eighteenth century. In his account of its history, Rev Neville Barker Cryer points to two distinct periods with an intermission in the 1740s when the last Jacobite rebellion in 1745 had divided the York brethren. A form of the Royal Arch was certainly being practised in York before 1740.[19]

Gould says that *the earliest known reference to the Royal Arch is in a report of a procession of members of the Lodge at Youghall, Co. Cork No.21 in 1743 when the Royal Arch was carried by two Excellent Masons.*[20]

In Dr. Fifield D'Assigny's rather verbosely titled *Serious and Impartial Enquiry into the Cause of the Present Decay of Freemasonry in the Kingdom of Ireland*, he also mentions Youghall. This indicates that the Royal Arch

---

18 Bernard E. Jones – *Freemasons' Royal Arch Guide*
19 *York Mysteries Revealed* – Rev Neville Barker Cryer
20 R.F.Gould – *The Concise History of Freemasonry*

certainly existed by that time and indeed there are reports of a Royal Arch Chapter at Stirling in Scotland back to that same year, although their earliest records are lost.

D'Assigny goes on to relate: *A certain propagator of a false system some few years ago, in this city (Dublin), who imposed upon several very worthy men, under a pretense of being Master of the Royal Arch, which he asserted he had brought with him from the city of York, and that the beauties of the Craft did principally consist in the knowledge of this valuable piece of Masonry. However, he carried on his scheme for several months, and many of the learned and wise were his followers, till, at length, his fallacious art was discovered by a Brother of probity and wisdom, who had some small space before attained that excellent part of Masonry in London, and plainly proved that his doctrine was false.*

This then tells us that the brother 'of probity and wisdom' had received the Royal Arch in London at some time prior to 1744. It certainly points to the Royal Arch being well established and known by then.

The other evidence we have is from a Mason called John Coustos (the son of a naturalised Englishman) who had set up in business as a jeweller in Lisbon. He was seized by agents of the Portuguese Inquisition, thrown into prison and tortured to make him reveal Masonic secrets. Some of what he revealed related to the Royal Arch – in 1743. Coustos was sentenced to the galleys but ultimately his brother-in-law in England secured his release.[21]

By this time there was dissension brewing. In something of an over-reaction to the multiplicity of exposures of Masonic ritual that were circulating in England – the most famous of which was Pritchard's *Masonry Dissect'd* of 1730 – the Premier Grand Lodge made some changes. Principal among these was the transposition of the words of the First and Second Degrees.

After Irish and Scottish Masons were refused entry to English lodges because they did not know what were now the correct words and a group of traditionalists accused the Premier Grand Lodge of turning away from the ancient landmarks, a rival Grand Lodge was set up in 1751 (although it was possibly 'on the drawing board' as early as 1739). The new Grand Lodge styled itself the Grand Lodge of England according to the Old Institutions or the 'Antients' on the basis that they were adhering to the traditional ways in which Masonry was done. They called the Premier Grand Lodge the 'Moderns' because they regarded them as innovators.

---

21   *The Freemason's Pocket Reference Book* by F.L.Pick and G.N.Knight

The full story of what happened is somewhat beyond our scope. It was not a schism because the majority of those who formed the Antients' Grand Lodge had not previously been Moderns. Suffice it to say it had a profound effect on the future of Masonry in general and the Royal Arch in particular.

The Charter of Compact and the Moderns' Grand Chapter

Beyond doubt, the Antients were very fond of the Royal Arch. Their first mention of it is in the minutes of their Grand Committee in 1752. Their Grand Secretary, the Irishman Laurence Dermott, described it as 'the root, heart and marrow of Freemasonry'. For that reason, they became friendly with the York Grand Lodge, whose geographical area was largely confined to Yorkshire but stretched a little into Lancashire and Cheshire. Very few Antients lodges were formed in this area. The Moderns were not so friendly to York but it is worth noting that they did have a Royal Arch Lodge (as they were then called) there, formed in 1762 as an offshoot of the Punch Bowl Lodge.[22]

The Moderns, though, were less sure about Royal Arch Masonry. Like the Antients they started off working the Royal Arch in their Craft lodges, but by 1765 an independent Chapter was meeting at the Turk's Head Tavern, Gerrard Street, Soho, on the second Friday of every month. It didn't have a name because lodges in those days tended to be referred to by the name of the tavern in which they met. The Chapter at the Turk's Head Tavern managed to attract the Grand Master of the Premier Grand Lodge into membership and Cadwallader, 9th Lord Blayney was exalted on 11 June 1766 (the term then used was 'Passing the arch') and immediately became First Principal.

Now, the word 'Chapter' suggests something a little superior, if not exclusive. It probably derives via the French word chapitre coming in turn from the Latin *capitutum* meaning of a head. It has been claimed that in assemblies of the great and good, such as in cathedrals and monasteries, meetings would be commenced with a reading from a chapter of the Bible and this is why we have the double meaning of the word. In the Church of England to this day, Deans and Chapters (assemblies of clergymen), convene in the cathedral's chapter house.

But the first Royal Arch bodies referred to themselves as Royal Arch lodges. And this term did not die out until early in the nineteenth century.

On 22 July 1766 it was determined by the Moderns to form the first Grand Chapter in the world which was known as the Excellent Grand and

---

22 *York Mysteries Revealed* – Rev Neville Barker Cryer

Royal Chapter of England, with Lord Blayney as First Grand Principal, a position he held for four years, three of which were after he had ceased to be Grand Master of the Moderns' Grand Lodge. The need to do this arose because there were objections in the Premier Grand Lodge to the working of the Royal Arch in Craft lodges, which was seen as an innovation.

For this reason the official position of the Moderns' Grand Lodge was anti-Royal Arch but the true situation was that many of the chiefs and rulers were, for whatever reason, joining it.

There is the famous instance of an Irishman, called William Carroll, who was in London in 1759 and fell on hard times. In ignorance, because he was not aware that the Grand Lodge of Ireland had lined itself up with the Antients, Carroll petitioned the Moderns' Grand Lodge for relief. The Grand Secretary of the Moderns, Samuel Spencer, gave him short shrift with the words 'Our society is neither Arch, Royal Arch, nor Antient' and referred him to the Antients' lodge at the Five Bells in the Strand. The Antients' Grand Secretary, Laurence Dermott, made much of this in a way that was rather typical of the sniping that went on between the two Grand Lodges at this time. Another example is Dermott's referring to the three irregular steps towards the pedestal in the First Degree as 'the drunkard's hornpipe'.

But having said all of that, Samuel Spencer had himself passed the Arch as he wrote those words, as did his successor, James Heseltine.[23]

So it was that on 22 July 1766, with nine seals and thirty signatures, the Charter of Compact was enacted and the Excellent Grand and Royal Chapter came into existence. The First Grand Principal, Lord Blayney, had been a Royal Arch Mason for forty days. The actual document did not become available until the following year.

For the moment there was just the Chapter at the Turk's Head; it was not until 1769 that subordinate chapters started to be warranted. By 1774 warrants were also being granted abroad.[24]

In a way it was somewhat ironic that the anti-Royal Arch Moderns had stolen a march on the Antients by forming the first Grand Chapter in the world. Dermott's reaction however was a calculated one. He claimed that the Royal Arch was simply the fourth degree of Craft Masonry and so no separate existence was necessary. And so it continued. But the Antients nonetheless formed a Grand Chapter in 1771 (although it did not actually

---

23 *The Premier Grand Lodge and the Delayed Recognition of the Royal Arch* by Roy Wells AQC82 (1989)
24 *The Origin and Development of Royal Arch Masonry* by Anthony R. Ough – The Batham Royal Arch Lecture for 1991 AQC 108 (1995)

meet until 1783) but this was largely window-dressing because it never amounted to any more than a committee of the Antients' Grand Lodge.

Some Chapters were called 'encampments', a collective name said to be derived from the encampments of the tribes of Israel. It was also quite common for the Royal Arch to be conferred on Sundays. Despite their official disapproval, by 1796 the Moderns had 104 Chapters.

The Situation in the Late Eighteenth Century

Problems then arose from without Masonry.

By the last decades of the eighteenth century a particularly volatile political atmosphere had arisen across Europe. Many people had seen revolution bring about significant change in America and France and wanted to try some of it. There was unrest in Ireland where the Society of United Irishmen fomented a revolt in 1798, in which Masonic Lodges had been used as a cover for rebellious activities. This ended with a French invasion which was a failure and with the Act of Union with Ireland in 1801.

There were also societies in England and Wales which were at least perceived to be fomenting unrest and attempts were made to link Freemasonry to this activity. Two particular published works gave rise to concern. One was by a conspiracy theorist and former Mason called Professor Robison and entitled *Proofs of a Conspiracy* and the other came from France and was called *Mémoires pour Servir à l'Histoire du Jacobinisme*, written by Abbé Barruel. Both were effectively saying that there was an international Masonic-Illuminati plot to undermine governments and the Church and that it was controlled by an unknown 'superior' – a fiction which some people still believe today. Both authors eventually had the grace to admit that English Masonry was not involved in any of this but by then the damage was done.

The Conservative government of Pitt the Younger decided to do something about this and secret Parliamentary Committees reported back in March of 1799 to the effect that there was a clear and systematic design on the part of the French (this was of course the period of the Napoleonic Wars) and domestic traitors to undermine every arm of the British establishment, through the setting up of political societies, such as the London Corresponding Society, a reasonably moderate group of mainly artisans who wanted electoral reform and opposed the war with France, and the United Englishmen who modelled themselves on the United Irishmen and were a lot more radical. The latter group met in secret and had 'esoteric handshakes'. Whilst this sounds conducive to paranoia and probably has echoes of the phrase 'weapons of mass destruction' of which we heard so much not long ago, it was pointed out that these societies would endeavour through oaths of fidelity and secrecy to form a bond of union which would seek to overthrow the monarch, the government and indeed the whole establishment. The Government was obviously taking matters very seriously because, in addition to several Acts of Parliament, detention without trial was brought in and habeas corpus was suspended.

Contemporary critics claimed that these accusations were ludicrous. George Tierney, effective leader of the Foxite opposition, said that he had never seen a report submitted to the House of Commons which was so little backed by evidence and that the Unlawful Societies Act, if it became law, would grant undue power to the Crown and breed an army of spies and informers.

Clearly Masonry was not the target of the Act. It was aimed at covert political cells, such as the ones mentioned above, recruiting their membership from a labouring class who genuinely believed that the French Revolution had achieved something for the common man and were prepared to go along to meetings and pay a penny or so a time and to sing songs and drink toasts which the establishment considered seditious.

However, it soon became apparent that 'oaths of secrecy and fidelity' applied very much to Freemasonry and that Masonic lodges would come within the purview of the Act.

Francis Rawdon (1754-1826) Earl of Moira, and from 1817 Marquess of Hastings, was Acting Grand Master (today he would be called Pro Grand Master) of the Moderns between 1789 and 1813, during the Grand Masterships of the Duke of Cumberland, the Prince of Wales and the Duke of Sussex. In the atmosphere of intrigues and alliances which pervaded the political scene of the early 19th century, he was seen as representing the Prince of Wales' entourage.

Moira was a close associate of the Prince but there is insufficient evidence to show that he persuaded HRH to intercede with Pitt on behalf of Freemasonry, as has been claimed. Rather Moira himself dealt directly and with a great deal of foresight with Pitt and, in doing so obtained a tremendous advantage for Masonry over many other genuine and innocuous organisations who found themselves banned. Moira was joined in his efforts by the 4th Duke of Atholl, Grand Master of the Antients, and together they successfully persuaded Pitt to exempt Freemasonry from the ban on oath-levying societies. In passing, it should be remembered that the Tolpuddle Martyrs were transported to Australia not for forming a trade union but for administering oaths. There was a proviso which was that all lodges should submit a return to the Clerk of the Peace for their area showing a list of their members with addresses and other personal data, as well as details of where and when the lodge met. This was accompanied by what looked like a ban on forming any new lodges and, as Frederick Smyth points out, this led to a brisk trade in warrants of failed lodges being bought by new lodges.[25] Amphibious Lodge No.258 in the Province of Yorkshire (West Riding) is an example of this. The lodge started at Stonehouse Barracks in Plymouth in 1786, failed possibly because all or most of the members went off to the Napoleonic Wars and was then revived in Yorkshire in 1803. The Province of West Lancashire still retains copies of the returns to the Clerk of the Peace, which continued to be sent in until 1967, and they are an absolute boon to lodge historians!

Working together on persuading Pitt to continue to allow Masonic meetings gave the two rival Grand Lodges an impetus to resolve the differences between them and attempts started to be made to bring about a union.

Articles of Craft Union were agreed and signed by both Grand Masters and their Committees at Kensington Palace on 25 November 1813 and were then ratified by both Grand Lodges. They were of such importance that for many years they were carried into every Grand Lodge meeting by the Grand Registrar.

It is fair to say that there were two unions effected on 27 December 1813. We know there was the Union of the Antients and the Moderns Grand Craft Lodges but by the often-quoted article two:

Pure and ancient Masonry consists of three degrees and three degrees only: those of Entered Apprentice, Fellowcraft and Master Mason including the Supreme Order of the Holy Royal Arch.

A further union thus came into being: that of the Royal Arch with the Craft. The former was now an integral part of the latter without a separate existence. What happened then was that the Royal Arch went into a form of limbo until 1817 when there was a further union of Grand Chapters. This was in a way a false union because the Antients' 'Grand Chapter' was already, with several other degrees, an inherent part of their Craft Grand Lodge, which had ceased to exist, so in effect there was nothing to unite with!

As a result of the Craft Union of 1813, the United Grand Chapter of Royal Arch Masons of England was formed in 1817 by the union of the Moderns' Grand Chapter of 1766 and the 'Antients so-called Grand Chapter of 1771. Augustus Frederick, Duke of Sussex, the Grand Master of the United Grand Lodge, had been given full power to negotiate this union, and new Constitutions were adopted on 15 April 1817 but it took some time to have them published. All Chapters registered before 27 December 1813 were automatically recognised by the United Grand Chapter if they

---

25 *A Reference Book for Freemasons* by Frederick Smyth (QCCC 1998)

were attached to a regular warranted Craft Lodge. Those chapters which were not attached to a regular Craft lodge had to get attached because, in England, a Royal Arch Chapter cannot exist if it is not attached to an existing Craft lodge warranted by the Grand Lodge and bearing the same number (the name can be different). In Scotland, Canada and United States the Chapters are independent under their Grand Chapters. The act of Union did not authorise lodges to work the Royal Arch as it had been the case with the 'Antients' lodges before although, since the 1790s, even the Antients tried to restrict the making of Royal Arch Masons to their Chapters only. For some time after 1817 some Chapters were reluctant to attach themselves to a lodge, and some others had difficulties to find a lodge that would accept them, as a lodge could only have one Chapter attached to it. In 1822 ninety Chapters were still unattached. In addition, some chapters working in Scotland under English charters granted before the Union could not attach themselves to any Craft lodge and were allowed to remain unattached. The regulations of the United Grand Chapter of 1823 did not require any more than that a candidate for Exaltation must be a Master Mason of 12 months' standing.

We really know very little of what took place in the lead-up to the Royal Arch Union. Wholesale changes were being made which would not appeal to the conservative, traditionalist Masonic mindset. We are hampered by a lack of paperwork partly because when the Duke of Sussex died (like all the sons of King George III, deeply in debt), bailiffs raided his apartments at St. James's Palace and took away a lot of his papers – and with them quite possibly a lot of our history. Given the climate of the age, the poor communications, distances from London, not to mention rumours and distortions, the situation for Companions in their Chapters must have been chaotic. In circumstances such as those there will have been a great temptation to carry on as if nothing had happened and indeed for many years the former 'Antients' lodges that had conferred Royal Arch Degrees continued to do so, and many Chapters went on working without any warrant or charter. In fact not only were they working the Royal Arch but also the Mark and Passed Master Degrees well into the 19th century. They talked of the Royal Arch as the Fourth Degree, which of course is contrary to the Articles of Union.

An example of these continuing pre-Union practices is found in the minutes of St.George's Lodge of Harmony (now) No.32 in Liverpool, from the year 1830:

Bro Deane took the chair and opened in the 3 Craft Degrees, when Bro Henry Ripley was duly installed as WM in the Chair and invested and saluted accordingly after which Bro Deane closed the Craft Lodge, Bro Ripley retired and a Passed Masters lodge was opened by Bro Lucas. Bro Ripley was then introduced, duly prepared and was admitted to the Degree of PM, which lodge being closed he again retired and a Conclave of Super Excellent Masons being opened, he was re-admitted, passed thro' the Veils and duly raised to the Super Excellent Degree, the Conclave was then closed and a RA Chapter opened, upon which he with Bros E.G.Deane and Jno Molineaux Jnr were readmitted, duly prepared and exalted to the sublime Degree of H.R.A.M.[26]

Another good clue to what went on is obtained by looking at what was done by the breakaway Grand Lodge of Wigan, which existed from 1823 until 1913. The story has been told many times but the facts are briefly that a rebellion against the new conditions of Masonry following the Union in Liverpool fizzled out but the protagonists moved to Wigan (some twenty miles distant) where the Lodge of Sincerity No.486 and some other lodges were also unhappy with the outcome of the Craft Union. A rival Grand Lodge was set up and the lodges under it reverted to the Antients' practices and numbering. The complete story has been well told elsewhere but what is interesting for our purposes is that Sincerity (although it had been a Moderns' lodge before the Union) continued working the Royal Arch Degree and wearing Antients' regalia, some of which is illustrated in Eustace Beesley's long-out-of-print book.[27] It is interesting to note that the flap of the RA apron has the TH (Templum Hierosolyma) symbol on it, the body of the apron bears three equilateral triangles and the jewels show the Seal of Solomon (i.e. the present RA jewel) within an arch.

As to the form of the official Royal Arch ceremony then, Harry Carr says this:

As to the development of the ritual of the R.A., it is surprising to find that, allowing for inevitable expansions and gradual changes in style and presentation, the essential elements are much the same today as they were in the 1760s. The earliest evidence we have on the subject for that period indicates that the candidate, h ... w ... d, discovered a scroll which was found to contain the opening words of the Gospel of St. John, ' In the beginning was the Word . . .' The Sojourners enacted the story of the 'Discovery', and the remainder of the ceremony, like the ordinary Craft working of those days, consisted of a Catechism of some 18 to 20 questions and answers. This may be described as the R.A. ritual of the first period.

The second period covers roughly the years 1780 to 1835. In the Craft, this was the period of the greatest stylistic advance in the presentation of the explanatory and symbolical elements of the ritual. In the Royal Arch, the essence of the ceremony remained largely unchanged, but, instead of only 18 to 20 questions in the Catechism, there were now some 80 to 100 questions, with lengthy answers covering much of the

---

26 *A Guide to Masonic Symbolism* by the present author
27 Eustace B. Beesley – *The History of the Wigan Grand Lodge* – Manchester Association for Masonic Research.

material which is given nowadays in the Historical, Symbolical and Mystical Lectures. Much of our present-day material was already there, not as straightforward pieces of recitation, but in the form of Q. and A.

The Royal Arch Union could be described as a textbook example of the great British art of compromise. You had the former Moderns – not all of whom were completely at ease with the Royal Arch – and the former Antients who were wedded to it. Carr again:

The work seems to have been dominated by the Rev. G. A. Browne, sometime Grand Chaplain of the United Grand Lodge, who was singled out at one of the meetings with special thanks for his services. In November, 1834, the ceremonies were rehearsed and approved by Supreme Grand Chapter, and a Chapter of Promulgation was formed in 1835, for six months only, to work as a Chapter of Instruction and, in particular, to ensure uniformity of practice throughout the Order. It demonstrated the newly-approved forms of the Installation and Exaltation ceremonies in a whole series of meetings held from May to August, 1835, and in November, 1835, to avoid misconception, the Grand Chapter '. . . resolved and declared that the ceremonies adopted and promulgated by special Grand Chapter on the 21st and 25th of November, 1834, are the ceremonies of our Order which it is the duty of every Chapter to adopt and obey'. DOMATIC, ALDERSGATE, STANDARD and several other versions are all descended from the R.A. ritual of November, 1834.[28]

So, the situation for Royal Arch Masons post-1817 continued to be very confused. It has to be said that Grand Chapter itself was not helping matters much. Lodges were praying to be allowed to form Chapters and being kept waiting for Charters (in one case in Lancashire for nearly 20 years.)[29]

The name of United Grand Chapter was changed to Supreme Grand Chapter in 1821, and so it remains.

In the eighteenth century the ritual of the Royal Arch and indeed the Craft contained many Christian references. Phrases like 'Rose of Sharon' and 'Lily of the Valley' which refer to Christ and are still known in other Degrees, were dropped. Nor has all vestige thereof been effaced because, in many rituals, the Opening Ceremony starts with the prayer 'Almighty God, to whom all hearts be open all desires known and from whom no secrets are hid etc' which, with some modernisation, is the collect still used in Anglican services to this day. One

Seal of Solomon.

---

28 Harry Carr – *More Light on the Royal Arch*
29 St.John's Lodge No.348, Bolton quoted in *Freemasons' Book of the Royal Arch* by Bernard E. Jones

How did the Royal Arch get to us? **37**

of the principal symbols of the Degree is the equilateral triangle which has always been used to represent the Holy Trinity. We still have three Principals, three Sojourners, three syllables of the Sacred Name, three greater lights and three lesser lights. We will discuss this further in Chapter 8 under the Ceremony of Exaltation. I have also even heard the words from the New Testament at John 1:1 used in Chapters *'In the beginning was the Word etc'*. Nor is that the end of it because Masons don't like change. In fairness also there is something not right about the Sojourners finding the passage of Scripture from St.John's Gospel (written in about AD70) when searching in the vault centuries before Christ. This is obviously the influence of the Philostorgius account (see above) and is now being corrected with the opening words of the Torah, the Law of Moses.

The years 1834 and 1835 are key so far as Royal Arch Masonry is concerned. The requirement that the candidate be an Installed Master had already been dispensed with. Supreme Grand Chapter now required only that the candidate should be a Master Mason of at least twelve months' standing. Since 1893 this delay was reduced at four weeks as it still is now. It is singular that, even today, I hear experienced Masons telling their juniors that they should not join Chapter until they have been through the Chair of their Lodge. This is presumably some kind of historical hang-back and the Masons who are saying it do not know why they are doing so. It is also nonsense. To my mind, by the time a brother of the Craft gets to the position of Junior Deacon in his lodge, he should be thinking seriously about joining a Chapter, if not already in one.

The other major provisions of the 1834/5 re-jig were these:
- De-Christianisation
- The ceremony of the Passing of the Veils was officially dispensed with, although it continued to be practised in various places for some time.
- Properly organised ceremonies were introduced for the Installation of Principals.
- The Principals' Lectures (Mystical, Symbolical and Historical) were introduced.
- The delivery of the old Royal Arch lectures (shown in Chapters 10 and 11) by catechism ceased.

The Duke of Sussex himself was a great universalist and would probably have liked to see every Lodge and Chapter in the English Constitution doing exactly the same ritual, as is the case in Ireland were uniformity is enforced by Lodges and Chapters of Instruction which have a totally different function from their English counterparts, but this was not to be. The Sussex Ritual (which refers to the Duke rather than the county) was intended to be the norm but in time the other workings – Aldersgate, Domatic, Complete, Metropolitan, etc, with local variations came to be the norm. The same situation applies in the Craft and is indicative of English Masons liking their bit of latitude, even though it can lead to hair-splitting on occasions.

There have been other changes since. In 1893 the qualifying period for a Master Mason to be exalted was reduced to four weeks, as we have seen. The opening of the Chapter by the Principals alone with the other companions waiting outside was largely discontinued by resolution of Supreme Grand Chapter in 1902 (but was still being done in Cyprus until 1920). It is still in print as part of the Perfect Ceremonies of the Royal Arch. However, Neville Barker Cryer records that the private opening is being done to this day in at least one Chapter in Yorkshire.[30]

Between 1954 and 1956 there was a major reorganisation of the Royal Arch Regulations, the revision of which had not kept pace with the Craft.[31] A revision of the Royal Arch Regulations was therefore made in 1955-56 in order to adapt them to the present conditions, and to make them more compatible with the Craft Constitutions. The Order is managed by a representation from all private Chapters on the register and by the Grand Officers, present and past, with the Three Grand principals at their head. It is called the Supreme Grand Chapter of Royal Arch Masons of England and it meets every three months. First Principals, present and past, if still active members, represent the private Chapters. In addition, a Committee of General Purposes also meets quarterly and manages the finances of Grand Chapter, deals with applications for Chapter, and acts as Board of General Purposes. To qualify to be elected as Grand Officers the candidates must be First Principals, present or past, of a Chapter. The Grand Master of the Grand Lodge, if an Installed First Principal, shall be the First Grand Principal, but if he has not these qualifications the First Grand Principal shall be elected annually. In the same way, and if qualified, the Pro Grand Master is the Pro First Grand Principal, and the Deputy Grand Master is the Second Grand Principal (at the time of writing this is not the case, although the Assistant Grand Master is now Third Grand Principal). If they have not the qualifications, the First Grand Principal appoints the two others. The Grand Secretary of the Grand Lodge, the Grand Treasurer and the Grand Registrar occupy, if qualified, the corresponding offices in the Royal Arch. The First Grand Principal appoints the other Officers. Grand Superintendents and Grand

30 Neville Barker Cryer – *What do you know about the Royal Arch?*
31 Sir James Stubbs – *Freemasonry in My Life*

Inspectors are Grand Officers. A petition to the Grand Chapter for a charter for a new Chapter must be signed by at least nine Royal Arch Masons and must be accompanied by a majority recommendation by the Master, Wardens and members of a regular lodge to which the proposed Chapter will be attached. Theoretically, a complete Chapter consists of three Principals, two Scribes, Treasurer, Principal Sojourner and his two assistants, and other Officers and Companions, making up the number of seventy-two. If they are more members then the members in excess may not hold the staff of office. The Officers of a Chapter are appointed by the Principals, or elected according to the Chapter's rules, but the three Principals and the Treasurer must be elected. The Installation and Investiture of Officers are laid down in the by-laws as imposed by the Grand Chapter Regulations. The precedence of the Officers is the following: the Three Principals, Scribe E. or Secretary, Scribe N., Treasurer, Director of Ceremony, Principal Sojourner, Assistant Sojourners, Assistant Director of Ceremony, Organist, Assistant Scribe E., Stewards and Janitor. However, some Chapters stick to the old concept of the principal officers being three Principals, two Scribes, three Sojourners and the Janitor.

The 'Antients' rule stated that 'no chapter shall be convened to exalt a candidate to the degree of Holy Royal Arch Mason unless six regular and registered Royal Arch Masons are present'. More recent rules, including the Grand Chapter Regulations of 1955-56, indicate that no exaltation can take place if the Three Principals and at least six companions are not present, the quorum being nine.[32]

Around 1964/5 it was determined that Companions below the rank of Principal should be allowed to hear the Principals Elect take their obligations and also to hear the robe addresses. There were then drastic reforms in 1988 and again in 2004, the effects of which are still being felt.

The Mark Degree, as well as the Veils, having been considered no longer necessary as a prerequisite for the Royal Arch, is now administered by the Grand Lodge of Mark Master Masons of England and Wales and its Districts and Lodges Overseas, with headquarters at Mark Masons' Hall in St.James's Street, London. It now seems that the only argument against having it as a precursor to the Royal Arch is the independence of Grand Mark Lodge from the Craft.

---

32 Nullens' *Official History of Freemasonry*

CHAPTER 3

The Symbolism of a Royal Arch Chapter

BELOW LEFT:
In Liverpool Masonic
Hall, the Egyptian
Room is permanently
set out for Royal Arch
Chapters.

The late Roy Wells described Freemasonry as 'a system of morality, veiled in allegory and sometimes illustrated by symbols'. It is true to say that not every aspect or quality in Masonry is symbolised, although most are. It is also true to say that people have been known to read too much into symbols and see symbolism where perhaps others would not. Beyond doubt, the Royal Arch is very rich in symbolism and this is what we shall now look at, considering first of all the furnishings and equipment of our Chapters and the jewel we wear.

BELOW: The
Egyptian Room is
also rich in Egyptian
symbolism. Photos
courtesy of the
Province of West
Lancashire.

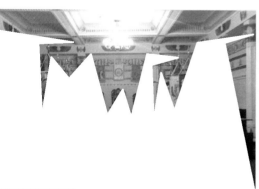

1. The Banners

The banners we see in our Chapters are divided into two groups – the four principal banners and the ensigns borne by the Companions on their staves.

The principal banners portray an ox, a man, a lion and an eagle. The sequence can always be remembered by the word omelette. As I have just proved, I do know how to spell O M E L E T T E and if you follow it logically the sequence would be ox, man, eagle and lion. However, it is a useful *aide-mémoire*.

So what is the significance of these four devices? Well, they can be found on the right-hand side of the arms of United Grand Lodge, which are an amalgam of the arms (or the crest because Grand Lodge did not apply for a grant of arms until 1918) of the Moderns' Grand Lodge on the left and the Antients' Grand Lodge on the right. The Moderns' Grand Lodge used the arms of the London Masons' Company which some say is where the Premier Grand Lodge came from. As we have seen above, the Antients attached a lot of importance to the Royal Arch and this is probably why they used these four devices.

But it goes back a lot further than that. In the vision of the prophet Ezekiel recorded in the Book of Ezekiel chapter 1 vv1-14 it says:

Now it came to pass in the thirtieth year, in the fourth month, in the fifth day of the month, as I was among the captives by the river of Chebar, that the heavens were opened, and I saw visions of God.

In the fifth day of the month, which was the fifth year of king Jehoiachin's captivity,

The word of the LORD came expressly unto Ezekiel the priest, the son of Buzi, in the land of the Chaldeans by the river Chebar; and the hand of the LORD was there upon him.

And I looked, and, behold, a whirlwind came out of the north, a great cloud, and a fire infolding itself, and a brightness was about it, and out of the midst thereof as the colour of amber, out of the midst of the fire.

Also out of the midst thereof came the likeness of four living creatures. And this was their appearance; they had the likeness of a man.

And every one had four faces, and every one had four wings.

And their feet were straight feet; and the sole of their feet was like the sole of a calf's foot: and they sparkled like the colour of burnished brass.

And they had the hands of a man under their wings on their four sides; and they four had their faces and their wings.

Their wings were joined one to another; they turned not when they went; they went every one straight forward.

As for the likeness of their faces, they four had the face of a man, and the face of a lion, on the right side: and they four had the face of an ox on the left side; they four also had the face of an eagle.

Thus were their faces: and their wings were stretched upward; two wings of every one were joined one to another, and two covered their bodies.

And they went every one straight forward: whither the spirit was to go, they went; and they turned not when they went.

As for the likeness of the living creatures, their appearance was like burning coals of fire, and like the appearance of lamps: it went up and down among the living creatures; and the fire was bright, and out of the fire went forth lightning.

And the living creatures ran and returned as the appearance of a flash of lightning.

Note, from the first verse, that this occurred during the time when the Children of Israel underwent their Babylonish captivity. Ezekiel, whose name means 'God strengthens' was taken into captivity when Nebuchadnezzar first invaded Judea and carried off King Jehoiachim and a large number of people in 597 BC. The prophet is being instructed to condemn the wickedness and idolatry of the Jewish people by this terrible vision of God, as a divine warrior, arriving on a chariot drawn by the four creatures. In a later vision, the prophet foresees the rebuilding of Jerusalem after her enemies have been destroyed and the erection of a new temple. The images of the ox, man, lion and eagle are revisited in the Book of Revelation chapter 4:

Coming from the throne are flashes of lightning, and rumblings and peals of thunder, and in front of the throne burn seven flaming torches, which are the seven spirits of God; and in front of the throne there is something like a sea of glass, like crystal. Around the throne, and on each side of the throne, are four living creatures, full of eyes in front and behind: the first living creature like a LION, the second living creature like an OX, the third living creature with a face like a HUMAN face, and the fourth living creature like a flying EAGLE. And the four living creatures, each of them with six wings, are full of eyes all around and inside. Day and night without ceasing they sing, 'Holy, holy, holy, the Lord God the Almighty, who was and is and is to come.' And whenever the living creatures give glory and honour and thanks to the one who is seated on the throne, who lives forever and ever, the twenty-four elders fall before the one who is seated on the throne and worship the one who lives forever and ever; they cast their crowns before the throne, singing, 'You are worthy, our Lord and God, to receive glory and honour and power, for you created all things, and by your will they existed and were created.'

Then again in chapter 7:

And all the angels stood round about the throne, and about the elders and the four beasts, and fell before the throne on their faces, and worshipped God.

These four figures have further significance because they are used to denote the four evangelists:

ABOVE LEFT:
The lion of St Mark

ABOVE RIGHT:
The eagle of St John

LEFT:
The Triple Tau
banner

ABOVE LEFT:
The ox of St Luke

ABOVE RIGHT:
The man of St Matthew

RIGHT: The tribe of Ephraim

ABOVE LEFT:
The tribe of Gad

ABOVE RIGHT:
The tribe of Simeon

LEFT:
The banner of the
tribe of Reuben

ABOVE LEFT:
The banner of the tribe of Zebulon

ABOVE RIGHT:
The banner of Assacher

RIGHT:
The banner of the tribe of Benjamin

ABOVE LEFT:
The banner of the
tribe of Manasseh

ABOVE RIGHT:
The tribe of Dan

LEFT:
The banner of the
tribe of Asher

The banner of the tribe of Naphtali   *The banner of the tribe of Judah*

Ox – St. Luke

Man – St. Matthew

Lion – St. Mark

Eagle – St. John

The origins of the symbols are connected to the opening imagery in their gospels. St. Matthew begins his account of the life of Christ by writing of his ancestry and so has as his symbol a winged man or an angel. St. Luke starts his book with Zachariah (father of St. John the Baptist) making a sacrifice in the Holy of Holies of the Temple, so he is shown with an ox, which is traditionally an animal used in religious sacrifice. St. Mark has the winged lion because he begins his account with St. John the Baptist 'preaching like a lion roaring'. St. John, who is symbolised by an eagle, starts with 'In the beginning was the word and the word was God'. The eagle is the animal which soars the highest in the sky and was reputed to be able to look directly into the sun with open eyes.

For this reason the city of Venice has adopted the lion, given that St. Mark is its patron saint.

The ritual tells us that the ox denotes the ministrations of patience and industry (or assiduity), the man personifies intelligence and understanding, the lion represents strength and power and the eagle indicates the promptness and celerity with which the will and pleasure of the Great I AM are always executed.

The principal banners are also said to represent the four seasons and also the elements. At one time, Jones believed, that the principal banners were three in number, bearing devices of a lion, a sceptre and a crown and placed behind the chairs of the Principals. If this is true, the practice was abandoned at the reorganisation of the ritual in 1835 when the present format was adopted.[33]

So that is why we have the principal banners but there is more to it than that. The banners of the Twelve Tribes of Israel when properly placed in a Royal Arch Chapter follow a sequence going from west to east thus:

Left-hand side	Right-hand side
Manasseh	Ephraim
Benjamin	Gad
Dan	Simeon
Asher	Reuben
Naphtali	Zebulon
Judah	Issachar

---

33 Bernard E. Jones – *Freemasons' Book of the Royal Arch*

We will look at these tribes in detail in a moment, but let me tell you another mnemonic for remembering them:

Left hand: My Brother Dan Almost Never Jumps
Right Hand: Every Good Sailor Rubs Zambuk In

Believe me, that information can come in very useful if you arrive for a Chapter convocation to find a pile of banners on the floor waiting to be erected!

As a further guide to what the banners look like (again in the same order) the legends on them are as follows:

Manasseh	a vine on a wall
Benjamin	a wolf
Dan	a horse and rider with a serpent biting the horse's heel*
Asher	a tree or cup
Naphtali	a hind
Judah	a lion couchant and sceptre**
Ephraim	an ox
Gad	a troop of horsemen
Simeon	a sword or crossed swords (sometimes with a tower)
Reuben	a man on a red ensign or waves to symbolise water
Zebulon	a ship in a haven
Issachar	an ass crouched between two burdens

*   There is sometimes an eagle in the background on the banner of Dan
**   *The sceptre shall not depart from Judah, nor a lawgiver from between his feet, until Shiloh come; and unto him shall the gathering of the people be.* Genesis 49:10 – note that Shiloh is the Messiah. Some versions of the Bible say a ruler's staff, rather than a lawgiver.

When the Children of Israel proceeded through the wilderness, this is the order in which they processed, with the Tribe of Judah leading and the Levites in the centre with the Ark of the Covenant. This order is also the one in which they pitched their tents as they stopped.

The Tribes were grouped under the banner of the principal Tribe in the group. Here, the four principal banners come into play again. The groups were as follows:

Group 1   on the eastern side: Judah with Issachar and Zebulon, under
          the banner of Judah – a lion

Group 2   on the southern side: Reuben with Simeon and Gad, under the
          banner of Reuben – a man

Group 3   on the western side: Ephraim with Manasseh and Benjamin,
          under the banner of Ephraim – an ox

Group 4   on the northern side: Dan with Asher and Naphtali, under the
          banner of Dan – an eagle.

So when we say in the Symbolical Lecture that the four principal banners
were the banners of the four divisions of the Army of Israel, we are only
really telling half the story.

The ritual used in describing these banners and the twelve tribes that
bore them is taken from the 49th chapter of the Book of Genesis and
their order is laid down in the second chapter of the Book of Numbers.
The ritual is rarely heard in most Chapters so I have reproduced it here.
It tells us this:

*1. The Banner of Judah was borne by Dashon its Prince. It was designated by a Lion
couchant surmounted by a Crown & Sceptre. Judah was the Chief Tribe, and was more
eminently distinguished, both for prosperity in war and peace and quietness at home. Its
dignity was marked by the Divine Favour, in choosing David from this Tribe to be the
Instrument of His Blessings to the people of Israel. To the Tribe of Judah was assigned
the most honourable station in the camp viz., in the East, before the Tabernacle, and
under its standard the Tribes of Issacher and Zebulon pitched their tents. The colour of
this banner is scarlet or crimson.*

*2. The Banner of Issachar was borne by the standard bearer of Prince Nethareel. It
was Sky Blue and was charged with a strong Ass crouching beneath its burden. The
ass is a patient animal and a proper symbol of labour. And accordingly, the prosperity
of Issachar sat quietly upon the land allotted to them and cultivated it with diligence
and assiduity. Instead of employing themselves in war or mercantile pursuits, they were
lovers of peace and quietness. The act of the ass couching between its burdens was an
apposite symbol of the indolent character of this Tribe, who would prefer a submission
to every species of tyranny and oppression rather than be at the trouble of asserting their
natural rights on the field of battle. Like the ass, which, though a strong and hardy
beast, would rather sink tamely under the heaviest load than shake it off by exertion of
its bodily powers.*

*3. Prince Eliab erected the Banner of Zebulon. It was Purple and bore for its
distinguishing characteristics a Ship. This was the prophecy of Jacob 'Zebulon shall*

dwell in the haven of the sea: and he shall be for a haven of ships: and his border shall be unto Zion'. [In point of fact the tribe of Zebulon dwelt inland.]

4. The device on the great Banner of Reuben, (Red or Scarlet) which was borne by Elizur, was another of the Cherubic forms viz., a Man, because Reuben was the first born of his Father, the 'excellence of dignity and excellence of power.' These Epithets may refer in general to the prerogatives of the first born, which Reuben would certainly have enjoyed according to his just claim, if he had not forfeited it by his offence. (He had slept with his Father's concubine and had also helped sell his brother Joseph into captivity). And therefore his Father predicted of him: 'Unstable as water thou shall not excel.' And then mentions the reason why, which means that, as water by a natural propensity inherent in its substance, flows from its source in an elevated situation to a place that is lower than itself, so should Reuben fall from his Birthright, and subside into an inferior situation among the Tribes. And that prophecy was remarkably verified, for nothing great or praiseworthy has been recorded respecting the posterity of Reuben. They were inferior in numbers to the other Tribes and the Pre-eminence was given to Judah.

5. Prince Shelumiel, as the leader of the Tribe of Simeon, bore a Yellow Banner emblazoned with a Sword (some say Simeon's Banner was emblazoned with a City or a Tower). Simeon and Levi were represented by instruments of war, the former with a Sword and the latter with a Dagger; in allusion to the abhorrence testified by the dying Patriarch of the city of these two sons, in the barbarous murder of the Shechemites, (their ruler's son had slept with their sister) under the assurance of kindness and good faith. Their father therefore said 'Cursed be their anger, for it was fierce; and their wrath, for it was cruel. I will divide them in Jacob, and scatter them in Israel.' Having been associated in wickedness, it was ordained by a superintending Providence that their posterity should be disunited that they not be furnished with an opportunity of working evil upon their brethren, after the example of their progenitors. Hence the Tribe of Simeon had little or no possession in the promised land, but dwelt in the midst of Judah; some of them wandered in search of a dwelling place as far as Mount Seir, and the deserts of Gideon. As for the Tribe of Levi, it was entirely dispersed among the tribes and devoted exclusively to the service of the Altar.

6. The Banner of the Tribe of Gad was under the charge of Prince Eliasaph. It was White and was emblazoned with a Troop of Horsemen. 'Gad signifies a troop; and was an allusion to the name that Jacob foretold the difficulties that would be opposed to the progress of his posterity by the hostility of their neighbours. But, though they were doomed sometimes to be defeated, yet in the end by divine assistance, they should overcome their difficulties and establish themselves firmly and peaceably in the portion allotted to them. This Prophecy was fulfilled to the letter; for the Tribe occupying a country beyond Jordan, were necessarily exposed to the incursions of the Ammonites, from whom they suffered severely; but at length, through the military talents of Jepthah, the Ammonites were finally subdued and troubled them no more.

7. Ephraim stepped into the inheritance of his Father Joseph and was elevated into one of the leading Tribes of Israel. His Green Banner, borne by Prince Elishama, was consecrated with the figure of a cherubic emblem of the Deity, viz., an Ox that denoted patient industry and strength. Thus Jehovah said, 'Ephraim is the strength of mine Head.'

8. Prince Gamaliel led the Tribe of Manasseh. Their tents were pitched under a flesh coloured Banner, which was charged with a luxuriant vine, planted by the side of a wall which its tendrils overhung. 'Joseph is a fruitful bough growing by a well watered soil, and shooting forth two luxurious branches.' This referred to the Tribes of Ephraim and Manasseh; and the prediction was fulfilled by their pre-eminence. Of Joseph it was said: 'The archers sorely grieved him, and shot at him and hated him: which referred to the persecutions of his Brethren who sold him into Egypt, to the false accusation by which he was thrown into prison. But 'his bow abode in strength, and the arms of his hand were made strong by the almighty God of Jacob.' As his enemies were termed Archers, so he is here said to be armed with a bow in his own defence, by which he triumphed over his enemies, and rose to the highest state of worldly prosperity.

9. Abidan, Prince of the Tribe of Benjamin, was designated by a Green Banner, emblazoned with a Wolf, because it was ever a warlike and cruel Tribe. It was predicted; 'Benjamin shall raven like a wolf in the morning he shall divide the spoil'. Though Benjamin was a great favourite of Jacob, as being his youngest son, yet he conferred no peculiar blessing on him, but describes him as the father of a fierce and warlike people. This is evident proof that Jacob acted under the influence of Divine inspiration. The Tribe accordingly partook of the character then depicted; they made war single-handedly against all the other Tribes, and overcame them in battle. Saul also, who sprang from this Tribe, possessed great military talents. His whole life was spent in war; and at length he, as well as his sons, was slain in battle.

10. The Tribe of Dan was the largest Tribe next to Judah, and it was for this reason probably that it was placed in the rear. The great Banner was borne by Prince Ahiezer. It was a Bright Green colour and charged with an Eagle, a component part of the Cherubim, denoting wisdom and sublimity. The name of Dan signifies Judging; and therefore Jacob said 'Dan shall judge the people'. Or in other words, that Tribe should be one head of one of the great divisions. He said further; 'Dan shall be a Serpent by the way', and that the Tribe of Dan was remarkable for defeating their enemies rather by policy than by force, of which there are many instances in the Bible. The Tribe of Dan, however, were ringleaders in idolatry and were the first who apostatized (forsook)

from God.

11. Prince Pagiel unfurled the Banner of Asher, which bore a flourishing Tree, or a Cup. Its colour was Purple. Asher's Tribe is promised a tract in the Holy Land, which should be fruitful and prolific, and accordingly it produced the necessaries of life in abundance and Mount Carmel abounded in the choicest fruits.

12. The Banner of Naphtali was borne by Prince Ahira, and was designated by a Hind. Its colour was Blue. 'Naphtali is a Hind let loose; he giveth goodly words'. This prophecy denotes that the posterity of Naphtali should be a spirited and free people; and that the Tribe should be fruitful and undergo a prodigious increase. And thus, from four sons, whom Naphtali brought with him into Egypt, proceeded upward of 50,000 descendants, when they were emancipated from their captivity. Their portion was in upper Galilee, a country always noted for the productivity of its soil. This agrees with the blessing which was given to the Tribe by Moses; ' O Naphtali, satisfied with favour and full with the blessings of the Lord,'

The Twelve Tribes of Israel have also been equated with the signs of the Zodiac, as follows:

REUBEN	AQUARIUS
SIMEON & LEVI	GEMINI
JUDAH	LEO
DAN	SCORPIO
NAPHTALI	CANCER
GAD	PISCES
ASHER	VIRGO
ISSACHAR	CAPRICORN
ZEBULON	LIBRA
EPHRAIM	TAURUS
MANESSEH	SAGITTARIUS
BENJAMIN	ARIES

We have seen that the formation we have was the order in which the Tribes proceeded when marching through the wilderness. Originally the banners in Chapters were set out in a square but nowadays they are in two columns.

In the end, the Tribes were dispersed throughout the land of Israel. Bernard E. Jones writes:

These tribes had been scattered throughout the length, but not much of the breadth, of

Palestine. In the extreme North, near Lake Meron, were Asher and Naphtali, south of them Zebulon, and to the east of the Sea of Galilee Manasseh. Much further south, below Manasseh, came Gad and at the extreme south, to the east of the Dead Sea, Reuben. The six other tribes were all west of the river Jordan: starting from the North, they were Issachar, next a branch of the tribe of Manasseh, then Ephraim, Dan, Benjamin (close to Jerusalem), and finally, on the west shore of the Dead Sea, Judah and Simeon.[34]

2. The Arch

'Mathematics resembles a well built Arch, Logic a Castle, and Romances Castles in the air' – Dean Swift

We call our Order the Holy Royal Arch Chapter of Jerusalem. We should perhaps look at the precise meaning of these words.

Q. *Why was your Chapter Holy?*

A. *Because we bless, praise and magnify the holy name of TTALGMH, our Chapter is set in the ruins of the Holy Temple of King Solomon and we advance towards the altar whereon the Sacred Name is engraved.*

Q. *Why was your Chapter Royal?*

A. *Because several Kings participated in the labour of temple building: Solomon, King of Israel and Hiram, King of Tyre joined with Hiram the widow's son in building the first temple. Cyrus King of Persia released the Children of Israel to return to their homeland and build the second temple and Zerubbabel, prince of the people, presided over that latter labour.*

Q. *What significance has the arch?*

A. *Beneath King Solomon's temple was a vaulted chamber containing nine arches and it was within the ninth of these that the Sacred Name was deposited.*[35]

We will return to the significance of the nine arches later.

Perhaps the first thing to do is define what an arch is.

A simple dictionary definition would be: a structure, especially one of masonry, forming the curved, pointed, or flat upper edge of an open space and supporting the weight above it, as in a bridge or doorway, or a masonry construction (usually curved) for spanning an opening and supporting the weight above it.

To get a bit more technical the *McGraw-Hill Dictionary of Architecture & Construction* defines an arch as: *A construction that spans an opening; usually curved; often consists of wedge-shaped blocks (voussoirs) having their narrower ends*

---

34 Bernard E. Jones – *Freemasons' Book of the Royal Arch*
35 See the Othello Catechism at Appendix 5.

toward the opening. Arches vary in shape, from those that have little or no curvature to those that are acutely pointed.

Encyclopaedia Britannica goes even further:

Its construction depends on a series of wedge-shaped blocks (voussoirs) set side by side in a semicircular curve or along two intersecting arcs (as in a pointed arch). The central voussoir is called the keystone, and the two points where the arch rests on its supports are known as the spring points. An arch can carry a much greater load than a horizontal beam of the same size and material, because downward pressure forces the voussoirs together instead of apart. The resulting outward thrust must be resisted by the arch's supports.

The thing to note is that in the case of the arch we are concerned with, it has a keystone. Not all arches have keystones. There are things that are set up purely for decorative purposes like the ones at Udaipur in India which are self-standing and so require no inherent strength, just the ability to remain upright:

Arches in some architectural styles don't have keystones either:

Even in England there are arches without keystones in the conventional sense:

So what is a keystone and why is it important? A dictionary definition again:

Keystone (also called headstone or quoin)

1. Architecture: The central wedge-shaped stone of an arch that locks its parts together. Also called headstone.

2. The central supporting element of a whole.

The word 'quoin', incidentally, can also be spelt 'coign' and equates to the modern French word *coin* meaning a corner.

Keystones go back a long way – in fact arches with keystones are said to have been used in ancient Thebes in 1500 BC, nearly five hundred years before the building of King Solomon's Temple:

So the keystone is important both in architectural terms because it is locking the other stones together to support the weight above it and in symbolic terms because it is, in the words of the Mark Degree, *'The most important stone in the building'*.

We can think of numerous examples of the symbolism of the keystone. Robert Burns in his poem *Tam O'Shanter* describes midnight as *'That hour of night's black arch the keystane'*.

We are taught in the Royal Arch ritual that the form of the Chapter approaches as near as circumstances will permit to a true catenarian arch. This is somewhat misleading because catenarian or catenary arches are

Moorish arches at the Alhambra Palace in Granada, Spain.

The remains of two arches at an ancient Greek temple.

merely chain-type arches, the principle of which was demonstrated to the Royal Society by Robert Hooke in 1671 in connection with the rebuilding of St.Paul's Cathedral, following the Great Fire of London.

The arch is also said to symbolise the Blue Arch of Heaven and the Rainbow which, as Royal Ark Mariners will know, represents God's covenant with mankind after Noah's flood. Mark Masons are also familiar with the importance of the keystone in that Degree and that is why, in many constitutions (but not the English), Advancement to the Degree of Mark Master Mason is a prerequisite for Exaltation into the Royal Arch.

In the Aldersgate Royal Arch ritual the address on the presentation of a Past Z jewel to a Past First Principal says:

Having passed the First Principal's Chair, you are deemed to have graduated in the whole Masonic system, from the Foundation Stone of Initiation to the Keystone of the Holy Royal Arch, and to have raised a structure perfect in its parts and honourable to the builder.

Our Chapters are laid out in the form of an arch, with the Three Principals at the eastern end, representing the keystone and two contiguous arch stones. Scribes Ezra and Nehemiah symbolise the two pillars of King Solomon's Temple and the rest of the Companions represent the columns supporting the arch with the Three Sojourners forming the base. When the candidate is being led round the Chapter during his Exaltation, the pattern of an arch should be described.

It could also be, of course, that by using the word 'arch' we are referring to superiority – as in Archbishop or Archdeacon. The Royal Arch has been referred to as a 'Capitular rite', and is still known as such in the United States. Capitular by definition means referring to a chapter, particularly an ecclesiastical one, and this implies that we are doing something a bit superior.

The Arch in a Royal Arch Chapter

The letters on the arch on the east side are the initials of the Three

Principals: Zerubbabel, Haggai and Joshua. On the west they spell out the words 'Fiat Lux' meaning 'Let there be light', coming of course from the third verse of the first chapter of the Book of Genesis and figuring on the scroll found in the vault.

The legend upon which the ceremony is based speaks of not one arch but nine supporting and enclosing a vault beneath the Temple of Solomon. This story is well known to Cryptic Masons, or members of the Order of Royal and Select Masters. Our RA ritual says:

The arch with its keystone at Temple Bar in London.

Early this morning on resuming our labours we discovered a pair of pillars (supporting an arch) of exquisite design and workmanship. Proceeding onwards we found six other pairs of equal symmetry and beauty.

Here presumably we are referring to the first seven of the nine arches, the final two having crumbled to dust. We learn that these arches are supporting the roof of a *'subterranean passage or gallery leading to that part of the Temple where the most holy place formerly stood. Our progress was here impeded by fragments which had fallen during the conflagration of the former temple'* (the last two arches?).

As we have seen, the Three Principals of a Chapter figuratively represent the keystone and two contiguous arch stones, which are wrenched forth during the ceremony of Exaltation.

The altar.

3. The Altar

The image right depicts a triangle, a circle and a square. They are interlinked and this is what effectively happens on the top of the altar which is a square plate of gold with a circle and triangle on top of it. Both these figures symbolise God; the circle because it is without beginning or end and the triangle because from ancient times the names of God were enclosed in triangular figures.

The equilateral triangle is a symbol of divine union, and was much revered by ancient nations as containing the greatest and most abstruse mysteries, and as a symbol of God, denoting a Triad of Intelligence, a Triad of Deity, a Triune God. Moreover, the Tetragrammaton, or incommunicable name was written by the Jews in a triangular form: the initial letter denoting the thought, the idea of God, a ray of light too transcendent to be contemplated by mortal eye. This name of God, the Tetragrammaton, could not be more aptly placed than in the symbol, or triangle, itself and hence the true meaning of the Royal Arch double triangle (see the Royal Arch jewel

below), originally represented thus, so that while this sacred emblem was deservedly revered by the Jews, both it and the double triangle itself are adopted as Royal Arch symbols.

The circle is an emblem of eternity having neither beginning nor end, and reminds us of the purity, wisdom, and glory of the Omnipotent, which is without beginning or end. It is also symbolic of friendship (as in 'circle of friends') and of moral virtues, as we look back to our Entered Apprentice Degree with the point within a circle bounded by two grand parallel lines.

The square represents the camp of the Israelites with the Ark of the Covenant in the centre representing the Blazing Star (see under the Banners above). Steinmetz held the opinion that the square symbolised the earth, and the circle and triangle the heavens.[36]

Until 1989, there was additionally a composite word in four languages – Chaldean, Hebrew, Syriac and Egyptian – with the following meanings:

1. His essence in majesty incomprehensible
2. I am and shall be
3. Lord in heaven or on high
4. Father of all

The old version of the Domatic ritual collected these into a little poem:

I am and shall be, Lord in heaven or on high,
'Father of all, in every age adored,
By saint, by savage and by sage,
Jehovah, Jove or Lord'

Some do quarrel with these translations but they are probably as near as we are going to get.

א   Aleph   ב   Beth   ל   Lamed

There were additionally three Hebrew characters on the plate of gold representing the letters Aleph, Beth and Lamed in the Hebrew alphabet.

---

36 George H. Steinmetz – *The Royal Arch: Its Hidden Meaning*

Those characters were also combined to form words meaning 'Father Lord', 'Word Lord' and 'Spirit Lord' – an obvious hark-back to the time when the Craft and the Royal Arch were exclusively Christian and a reference to the Holy Trinity. It is interesting that, using the numerical values assigned to Hebrew characters: aleph = 1, beth = 2 and lamed = 30, totalling 33 – the number of years of the life-span of Jesus Christ.

In Spain and in South America the Holy Trinity is sometimes portrayed by a figure representing God the Father with a triangle over its head, another representing God the Son with a halo, or circle, and then a dove to represent the Holy Spirit.

If I may make so bold, I very much regret that this part of the Exaltation ceremony was dropped. Unfortunately the late 1980s were a period of anti-Masonic sentiment and sections of the press and others with not enough to do had postulated (or rather revived because the Rev Walton Hannah, anti-Masonic author of *Darkness Visible* and *Christian by Degrees* first made this claim in the 1950s) the theory that this composite word was in fact the Masonic god, which of course was not, is not and never has been the case.

The Altar itself is a double cube. This is a complex mathematical problem as we shall see later. It is supposed to be made of marble, a symbol of purity and immortality and also of tradition and refined taste, and is fronted by the initials of the Three Grand Masters at the building of the First Temple. At one time it bore on one side the initial of the word of an Installed Master. This ceased with the amendments to the ritual made in 1835. The letters above therefore stand for Solomon, King of Israel, Hiram, King of Tyre and Hiram Abif but I have also seen them as SRI and HRT the middle letter standing for Rex, the Latin word for king. There is also of course the Triple Tau which appears below the initials of the three kings.

4. The Six Lights

Amongst the other equipment in a Chapter the Six Lights are very much interconnected with the Five Regular Platonic Bodies, the mysterious Triple Tau and the Royal Arch jewel (see overleaf).

There are three lesser lights and three greater lights which are specially arranged. They form, as the ritual tells us, a series of equilateral triangles which, when reduced to their amount in right angles, will be found equal to the Five Regular Platonic Bodies.

We go on to learn that the three lesser lights represent the *'light, the law and the prophets and by their number allude to the Patriarchal, Mosaical and Prophetical dispensations'*. What does this mean? It requires some explanation

The Altar in a Royal Arch Chapter.

because, although the ritual (Complete Working) does say *the Light, the Law and the Prophets, older rituals or those that originated from older rituals such as the Perfect Ceremonies say the Light OF the Law and the Prophets.* This makes a difference because we are asking to be enlightened by the Law, which means the five books of Moses (or the Pentateuch) – Genesis, Exodus, Leviticus, Numbers and Deuteronomy – and the Prophets, which are the books of the various prophets in the Old Testament each of whom received a command from God to pronounce His Holy Will and Word. The Patriarchal dispensation refers to God's commands to Abraham, Isaac and Jacob. The Mosaical is obviously Moses being told to lead the Children of Israel out of Egypt. The Books of the Prophets or the Prophetical dispensation refers to the longer prophesies of Isaiah, Jeremiah (including the Book of Lamentations), Ezekiel and Daniel, together with the shorter ones of Hosea, Joel, Amos, Obadiah, Jonah, Micah, Nahum, Habbakuk, Zephaniah, of particular interest to us Haggai, Zechariah and Malachi. Among many prophesies in these books concerning the backsliding of the Israelites and God's judgement of them, the advent of the Messiah or Christ and the destruction of Jerusalem are also foretold.

The greater and lesser lights surround the Altar.

Next we are taught that the three greater lights *'represent the Sacred Word itself and the Triune Essence of the Deity and are emblematic of His creative, preservative and de-creative powers'*.

We will consider the arrangement of these lights further when we look at the Lecture explaining the Companion's jewel in Chapter 9.

5. The Five Regular Platonic Bodies

These are usually found on the floor of the Chapter, in front of the Altar. The Hexahedron is of course a cube and the Tetrahedron is a pyramid.

The Five Regular Platonic Bodies are, in geometric terms, regular polyhedrons. The word polyhedron comes from two Greek words meaning 'having many faces'. The faces of the Platonic bodies are congruent, in other words all the faces of the bodies are of the same size. The five are illustrated above and take their names from the Greek words for the number of sides of each: the Tetrahedron has four sides, the Hexahedron (or cube) has six, the Octahedron eight, the Dodecahedron twelve and the Icosahedron twenty.

Although these solids are called Platonic, there is evidence that they were studied in Neolithic Scotland some 1000 years before Plato and the models they made then can be seen in the Ashmolean Museum in Oxford. Some claim Pythagoras had more to do with their discovery. They certainly fascinated the Ancient Greeks and Plato wrote about them in the *Timaeus* in 360 BC.

Five Regular Platonic Bodies

Plato it was who associated these bodies with the four elements of the universe: earth, fire, air and water, and the sphere in which the universe is housed. Euclid, Aristotle and Johannes Kepler later expanded on this theory. Modern chemistry reckons elements in the universe by the Periodic Table.

Fine, but what do we use them for?

As we shall see again when considering the Royal Arch jewel, the solids represent the four elements and the sphere of the universe thus (in the order from left to right in which they should be laid out):

Tetrahedron = fire

Octahedron = air

Cube = earth

Icosahedron = water

Dodecahedron = the sphere of the universe

Jerusalem Cross.

A mnemonic for remembering the order of the Platonic bodies is T O C I D. Unfortunately, because some Chapters do not possess Platonic bodies, they are not referred to in the Symbolic Lecture, but they do figure largely in the explanation of the jewel worn by the Companions.

There is also a connection with the mysterious Triple Tau as we shall see below.

6. The Mysterious Triple Tau

Tau is the last letter of the Hebrew alphabet, very much as Omega is the last letter of the Greek alphabet and we refer to God in the explanation of our signs as the 'Alpha and Omega' – the beginning and end. Similarly the Tau symbolises finality. It is also the nineteenth letter of the Greek alphabet.

Triple Tau.

Initially the Tau in the Royal Arch appeared as a T superimposed on an H and was said to represent *Templum Hierosolyma* – the Temple at

Jerusalem. Early Royal Arch aprons have those two letters as a centrepiece.

In the Mystical Lecture we describe the Tau as *'derived from the Hebrew, it is that mark or character spoken of by the angel whom Ezekiel saw in the spirit when it was said to the man with the writer's inkhorn "Go through the midst of the city, through the midst of Jerusalem, and set a mark on the foreheads of men that sigh and that cry for all the abominations that be done in the midst thereof."'*

The ritual goes on to tell us that those who had the mark on them were *saved from among those slain for their idolatry by the wrathful displeasure of the Most High,* that it was also placed on those who has been acquitted by their judges and by military commanders on those who had returned from the field of battle unharmed. We are also told that the Tau has ever been considered a mark or sign of life.

As a matter of interest, whereas the Tau is considered a sign of life, the eighth letter of the Greek alphabet – theta Θ – represents death and it from these two characters that some say our plus (+) and minus (–) signs are derived.

As another aside, the Tau is sometimes referred to as the St. Anthony's cross because the saint was crucified on a cross of that shape.

Up to now we have been talking about the Tau on its own but we go on to learn that the union of the Triple Tau alludes to the *Grand Triune of the Deity by whom the gloomy, horrific and unshapen chaos was changed into regular form and peaceful existence.*

So the Triple Tau is another symbol of God.

Tau crosses, of course, appear all over the place. In many Christian organisations a four-way tau is used to represent both the spreading of the Gospel (by the smaller crosses emanating from the big one) and the five wounds of Christ. It is also said to symbolise by the Tau cross the law of Moses and its fulfilment by the four Greek crosses in Jesus Christ.

The number of right angles in the Triple Tau which is two at each of its exterior lines and two at their union in the centre relates to the Five Regular Platonic Bodies discussed above. The number of right angles in each body divided by four gives the number of Triple Taus in that body thus:

Tetrahedron – four right angles = 1 Triple Tau = fire
Octahedron – eight right angles = 2 Triple Taus = air
Cube (or Hexahedron) – twelve right angles = 3 Triple Taus = earth
Icosahedron – 20 right angles = 5 Triple Taus = water
Dodecahedron – 36 right angles = 9 Triple Taus = the sphere of the universe

We will return to the Tau later when we consider the Royal Arch jewel.

7. The Pick, Crow and Shovel

These may rightly be termed the working tools of the RA Degree, as the implements made use of by the Sojourners who went to clear the ground for the foundation of the Second Temple. The Symbolical Lecture describes these tools in accordance with their practical uses: the pick to loosen the earth, the crow to make purchases and the shovel to clear away the loose earth and rubbish.

The Symbolical Lecture goes on to spiritualise these implements as follows:

The stroke of the Pick reminds us of the sound of the last trump when the grave shall be shakened and loosened and give up its dead; the Crow being an emblem of uprightness points out the erect manner in which we shall rise on that awful day to meet our tremendous, though merciful, judge; while the manner in which the body is laid in the grave is depicted by the work of the shovel for we may, with firm but humble confidence, hope that when these earthly remains shall have been properly disposed of, the spirit may arise to immortal life and everlasting bliss.

The use of these implements in the Royal Arch ceremony dates back to the 18th century and there is little symbolism attached to any of them outside Masonry. I suppose their use is just logical as the sort of tools one would need to do the particular job in hand.

8. The Bible, Square and Compasses

The ritual tells us that *the Bible, Square and Compasses are intended to represent the Three Grand Masters who bore sway at the building of the First Temple at Jerusalem. The Bible represents the wisdom of King Solomon, the Square the strength of King Hiram of Tyre and the Compasses the curious and masterly workmanship of Hiram the Widow's Son. It goes on to say that these objects also represent the wisdom, strength and beauty of God in that His wisdom is exemplified by the Volume of the Sacred Law, His*

The Bible, Square and Compasses

strength by the Square – the criterion of perfection – and His unerring and impartial justice by the Compasses.

Two things strike me about this passage. One is that we refer to the Sacred Volume as the 'Bible' which is curious given that the Royal Arch is not restricted to Christians. In my Chapter many of the candidates take their obligation on the Koran. The other is that we are involved in completing what has been called the 'ultimate step' in Freemasonry and we are bringing with us the Three Great Lights of the Craft.

9. The Sceptres

These are carried by the Three Principals and, we are told in the Symbolical Lecture, symbolise the regal (Zerubbabel – a crown), prophetical (Haggai – the all-seeing eye) and sacerdotal (Joshua – a bishop's mitre) offices. It has been suggested that the seniority of our Principals is wrong and that Joshua should come before Haggai in the sequence Prophet, Priest and King. The logic behind this contention is partly to do with the life and mission of Jesus Christ who first prophesied, then through His supreme sacrifice performed the priestly function and finally ascended into Heaven where He lives and reigns as King. It is interesting to note that, in an Irish Chapter (see Appendix 3), the High Priest is in the Second Principal's position after the Excellent King or First Principal.

The sceptre top bearings are miniature versions of the hats still worn in some Chapters as we shall see in chapter 4. The Three Principals salute their sceptres at the beginning of each convocation and mentally repeat the word of their chair.

10. The Royal Arch Jewel

We enter now into what is a very complex area of Masonic science. We have a jewel with several mottoes on it. Three of those mottoes are in Latin, which is a language no longer as extensively taught in the British education system as it was in the 18th and 19th centuries. One of them

The Sceptres of the First, Second and Third Principals in order.

is partly in Greek and partly in Latin. There is a further motto which is in English.

Let's look at these mottos – the Latin ones first:

1. *Nil nisi clavis deest.* This phrase, meaning 'Nothing is wanting but the key' is first encountered in the works of John Dee (1527-1608) who was a Rosicrucian and an alchemist, as well as being mathematician to Queen Elizabeth 1. These words are engraved around a scroll at the bottom of the jewel, in which is contained the Triple Tau, as if to confirm what we have already said – that the Tau is the key to unlocking the mysteries of the Royal Arch.

2. *Si talia jungere possis sit tibi scire satis* – If thou canst comprehend these things, thou knowest enough. This is another one with roots in alchemy.

3. *Deo, regi, et fratribus, honor fidelitas, benevolentia* – For God, king, and brethren; honour, fidelity, and benevolence. This, so far as I can tell, is a Masonic axiom derived from the Regius Poem, the oldest 'charge' of them all, dating to the 14th century and in the possession of Grand Lodge:

Royal Arch jewel.

> *That whoso will con this craft and come to estate,*
> *He must love well God and Holy Church algate,*
> *And to his liege Lord the King*
> *To be true to him o'er alle thing*
> *And thy fellows thou love also*
> *For that the craft will that thou do.*

This covers nicely the words used in the motto. The archaic word 'algate' simply means at all times or in all ways.

The two mottoes above (2 and 3) are engraved around and within two concentric circles on the jewel, one at the front, the other at the back. The circles themselves represent God (the inner) and eternity (the outer).

Then the motto that is partly Greek, partly Latin:

4. **ΕΥΡΕΚΑΜΕΝ** (pronounced Eurekamen or Evrekamen) *Invenimus cultor dei civis mundi* – We have found the worship of God, O citizen of the world. The Greek word is of course familiar to us as what Archimedes shouted when he jumped out of his bath having discovered how ships float. It is engraved across the two intersecting triangles represented in the centre of the jewel.

Finally, the English one:

5. Wisdom, strength, beauty, peace, concord, truth.

Before considering the interlaced triangles on which these words appear, we need to look at the centre of the jewel which is sometimes a little hard to make out. There is a triangle, again the symbol of the triune God, within which is an irradiated sun issuing a pair of compasses, below which is a globe representing the earth.

The use of the Greater and Lesser Lights and the Five Regular Platonic Bodies (see above) in explaining the structure of the RA jewel is extremely complicated, especially for those of us who are not mathematicians. The late Harry Carr was quite scathing in his criticism of the explanations:

Personally, I find them quite incomprehensible, and wholly irrelevant to the teachings of the RA. Even if the explanations were complete and correct I would not mourn their passing, because I believe it is our duty to instruct and enlighten Candidates, not to confuse them with matters which can only be understood by specialists and which have no genuine place in our teachings.[37]

However, let us persevere.

The words *Nil nisi clavis deest* (Nothing is wanting but the key) are important because what they are saying is that the Triple Tau acts as a key to open the Royal Arch jewel and that this is rationale behind the connection of the Triple Tau, the Royal Arch jewel, the Five Regular Platonic Bodies and the four elements and the sphere of the universe.

We have now looked at the mottos on the jewel and what they mean. In Chapter 9 we will look at the Lecture explaining the jewel and its geometric properties.

---

[37] Harry Carr – *The Freemason at Work*

CHAPTER 4
The Three Principals

Note: a picture of Three Principals in hats appears on the Kirkwall Scroll held by Lodge Kirkwall Kilwinning No.38 on the Orkney Islands. Cooper points out that, while carbon-datings have placed that scroll in the 16th century, the references on it to matters associated with the Third Degree mean that the images cannot have been created on the scroll before 1720 when the Third Degree began to appear in Scotland (in fact the Lodge of Aitcheson's Haven did not start working it until 1814).[38]

Hats are also worn in the Chapter of Sincerity No.600 in Bradford, West Yorkshire. In most Chapters today the hats are abandoned but their appearance is retained in the tops of the Principals' sceptres.

A Royal Arch Chapter is ruled by three Principals. This rule is joint, very much more so than the government of a Craft lodge by the Master and his two Wardens. For example, the Address to the Master is a very special part of the Craft ceremony of Installation, but at a Chapter Installation the Three Principals are addressed together. The First Principal or MEZ is nonetheless *primus inter pares* because as the Warrant of a Craft lodge is delivered to the new Worshipful Master at his installation, the Charter of a Chapter is delivered specifically to the MEZ, together with the Royal Arch Regulations and Chapter by-laws.

The First Principal of a Royal Arch Chapter represents Zerubbabel, Prince of the People. Hence his jewel is an irradiated crown within a triangle.

So who was Zerubbabel?

Zerubbabel (sometimes written Zorobabel) means 'one sown of Babylon'. He was a grandson of Jehoiachim, the King of Judah whom Nebuchadnezzar, King of Babylon took into captivity. He is referred to in the ritual as the son of Shealtiel, but this is disputed and he may have been his nephew.

Jewel of First Principal.

After Cyrus the Great released the Jews and allowed them to return to Jerusalem to rebuild their Temple, Zerubbabel led the first wave of returnees at some time between 538 (the first year of the reign of Cyrus, King of Persia) and 520 BC. In this first wave 42,360 Jews returned and they were also allowed to bring back the sacred vessels that Nebuchadnezzar had confiscated. Zerubbabel is always strongly associated with Joshua, the son of Josedech, the high priest, who also led the Jewish return.

In 522 BC Cyrus was succeeded by Darius 1, who appointed Zerubbabel Governor of the Persian Province of Judah. It was then that the rebuilding of the Temple started.

Zerubbabel is mentioned in many books of the Bible: 1 Chronicles, Ezra, Nehemiah, Haggai and Zechariah. He also appears in the Apocryphal books of Esdras and Sirach. Haggai prophesied that Zerubbabel, who was of the line of King David, would become King of the Jews:

'On that day, says the Lord of Hosts, I will take you Zerubbabel, son of my servant, and wear you like a signet ring for it is you whom I have chosen. This is the word of the Lord of Hosts.' (Hag. 2:23)

The seal or signet ring was an indication that the wearer was God's representative on earth. A signet is a ring on which there is a device or impression, common among the ancients as a symbol of authority and often used for making impressions on important documents and as such it would have had the status of a royal decree. A signet would generally be worn on the index finger of the right hand.

The Signet of Zerubbabel does not figure in English Royal Arch ceremonies as it does elsewhere but it is important because it is also known as the 'Signet of Truth'. There is a story which forms part of the Degree of Red Cross of Babylon in the Order of the Allied Masonic Degrees where Zerubbabel returning to the court of King Darius is asked which is greater: the strength of wine, the power of the king or the influence of women. Zerubbabel replies that truth is stronger than all the other things and hence his signet is also known as the Signet of Truth.

He was certainly a great man, although nothing is known of his end. He was succeeded by his son and grandson as Governor of Judah.

The Second Principal represents Haggai the Prophet, symbolised by the All-seeing Eye.

Jewel of Second Principal.

Haggai was one of twelve minor prophets in the Old Testament and, with Zechariah and Malachi, he prophesied at the time of the return of the Jews from Babylon. It must be stressed that not all the Jews wanted to return because many of them had established thriving businesses in Babylon, particularly in the financial sector. Cyrus did not force any of them to return, he just wanted to give them that choice.

Haggai did not begin his ministry until 16 years after the first return, by which time the work on rebuilding the Temple had been suspended and lethargy had set in. Haggai, with Zechariah, urged the Jews to do God's work and make that their first priority, rather than worrying about worldly things.

Haggai's name means 'holiday' (as in holy day) and he is thought

to have almost definitely been the author of the Book of Haggai. The book is a short one, comprising four oracles in two chapters with a total of 38 verses. The first eight verses of chapter two are what are read in the ceremony of Exaltation. Almost nothing is known of Haggai as a person or how and when he died. As we have seen, he prophesied that Zerubbabel would be King of Israel and that the line of Davidic kings would be restored but modern scholars have cast doubt on this.

The Prophets.

The Third Principal represents Joshua, the son of Josedech, the High Priest. The Book of Zechariah chapter 6, verses 9–13 says this:

Heldai, Tobijah, and Jedaiah have returned from Babylonia. Collect enough silver and gold from them to make a crown. Then go with them to the house of Josiah son of Zephaniah and put the crown on the head of the high priest Joshua son of Jehozadak. Tell him that I, the LORD All-Powerful, say, 'Someone will reach out from here like a branch and build a temple for me. I will name him "Branch", and he will rule with royal honours. A priest will stand beside his throne, and the two of them will be good friends.

Jewel of Third Principal.

Joshua was the first High Priest after the return from captivity in Babylon and served in that capacity, alongside Zerubbabel, for a number of years. He did not write a book and his scripture reading during the ceremony of Exaltation is taken from Proverbs. He is said in the Book of Zechariah to have experienced a vision that told him how to run the priesthood and the Temple. It was claimed in 1825 that his tomb had been found near Baghdad which implies that he returned to Babylon at some point.

Now, before considering the role of the Principals, let us look at the functions of the officers of a Royal Arch Chapter generally. These are summarised in an old Yorkshire ritual as follows :

Z: Companion Scribe Nehemiah, of how many officers does a Royal Arch Chapter consist?

SN: Nine, Most Excellent.

Z: Name them.

SN: Three Principals, Two Scribes, Three Sojourners and a Janitor, Most Excellent.

Z: What is the situation and duty of the Janitor?

Scribe Ezra: Without the door of the Chapter, Most Excellent, to guard its approaches so as to prevent intrusion and the profanation of our mysteries.

Z: Companion 2nd Assistant Sojourner, what is your situation and duty?

2nd Asst. Soj: At the left of the Principal Sojourner and, in conjunction with the 1st Assistant Sojourner, to aid and assist him in his duties, Most Excellent.

Z: Companion 1st Assistant Sojourner, what is your situation and duty?

1st Asst Soj: At the right of the Principal Sojourner, to aid and assist him in his duties, Most Excellent.

Z: Companion Principal Sojourner, what is your situation and duty?

PS: In the west, Most Excellent, to examine candidates and afterwards to prepare them for and conduct them through the ceremony of Exaltation.

Z: Companion Scribe Nehemiah, what is your situation and duty?

SN: At the door within the Chapter, Most Excellent, to receive candidates for Exaltation, in due form, announce the approach of Companions, and to assist the Scribe Ezra in the ceremonial duties of his office.

Z: Companion Scribe Ezra, what is your situation and duty?

SE: In the south, Most Excellent, to issue summonses, record the transactions of the Chapter, and perform the ceremonial duties attached to my office.

Z: Excellent Companion Third Principal, whom do you represent?

J: Joshua, the son of Josedek, the high priest, Most Excellent.

Z: Your duty?

J: To aid and assist in carrying on the Lord's work, Most Excellent.

Z: Excellent Companion Second Principal, whom do you represent?

H: Haggai, the prophet, Most Excellent.

Z: Your duty?

J: To aid and assist in completing the Lord's work, Most Excellent.

Z: Excellent Companion Past Principal, what is the situation of the First Principal?

PP: On the throne in the east, Most Excellent.

Z: Whom does he represent?

PP: Zerubbabel, Prince of the people.

Z: His duty?

PP: To conduct the proceedings of the Chapter according to the Grand Original, Most Excellent.

Although the phrase 'Grand Original' in the last line is a little unclear and could mean a number of things, this is a pretty good summation of the duties of the Principal Officers of a Chapter. The only thing that will be unfamiliar to many of us is the situation of the Scribe Ezra, who normally sits in the north, where the Secretary would sit in a Craft lodge. In some Chapters also, the Scribe Nehemiah sits in the south.[39]

At Royal Arch banquets it is customary to toast the 'Grand Originals'. The colloquy between the First Principal and the Principal Sojourner is well known but it is worth noting that the manner of reciting or reading, proposing and honouring the toast is probably the last vestige of the 18th century way of doing all Masonry, in catechetical form all seated round a table.

The Third Principal in a few remaining Chapters wears a High Priest's breastplate. In the Chapter of Sincerity at Bradford (referred to above) the following address is given to the newly installed Third Principal:

'This breastplate with which you have been invested is a replica of that made by Aaron the first High Priest, to be worn by him on great and solemn occasions. The linen cloth has four squares bearing four rows of precious stones set in pouches of gold, twelve in all and each stone having engraved thereon the name of one of the tribes of Israel.

It was called the breastplate of judgement and later of righteousness, of faith and love. It is meant to remind you of your obligation to be obedient to our laws and regulations, and that the welfare and happiness of your Chapter should ever be engraven on your heart.'

The colours of the stones should therefore correspond with the colour of each tribe's banner.

The Scribe E of the Chapter, Ex.Comp John Watson tells me: *'I did find in the Chapter Centenary booklet that the three crowns and breastplate were purchased in October 1899 at a cost of £15–6–6, together with a box to hold them which cost a further £1–15–0. These are still in use today. According to the inflation calculator on the Bank of England website £17 in 1899 would be over £1,800 in today's money!'*

So what then was the breastplate and what purpose did it serve?

As will be seen from the illustration below, the breastplate has twelve stones set in it to represent the 12 tribes of Israel as follows:

Reuben – the Odem or ruby

Simeon – the Piteda or topaz

Judah – the Nofech or turquoise

---

39 Aire and Calder (Goole) Chapter No.458, ritual compiled in 1929

Issachar – the Sapir or sapphire
Zebulon – the Yahalom or diamond
Dan – the Leshem or jacinth
Naphtali – the Shvo or agate
Gad – the Ahlama or jasper
Asher – the Tarshish or emerald
Benjamin – the Yashfe or jade

That leaves, according to our Royal Arch list of tribes, Ephraim and Manasseh who were the sons of Joseph who is symbolised by the Shoham or onyx. The Temple Mount Faithful website also includes the tribe of Levi who are excluded from our list because of their part in the barbarous murder of the Shechamites but are represented by the Bereket or beryl.[40]

These stones were not chosen at random but dictated by God as we read in Exodus 28 vv1–43:

The Priestly Garments

Have Aaron your brother brought to you from among the Israelites, along with his sons Nadab and Abihu, Eleazar and Ithamar, so they may serve me as priests. Make sacred garments for your brother Aaron to give him dignity and honour. Tell all the skilled workers to whom I have given wisdom in such matters that they are to make garments for Aaron, for his consecration, so he may serve me as priest. These are the garments they are to make: a breastpiece, an ephod, a robe, a woven tunic, a turban and a sash. They are to make these sacred garments for your brother Aaron and his sons, so they may serve me as priests. Have them use gold, and blue, purple and scarlet yarn, and fine linen.

The Ephod

Make the ephod of gold, and of blue, purple and scarlet yarn, and of finely twisted linen – the work of skilled hands. It is to have two shoulder pieces attached to two of its corners, so it can be fastened. Its skillfully woven waistband is to be like it – of one piece with the ephod and made with gold, and with blue, purple and scarlet yarn, and with finely twisted linen.

Take two onyx stones and engrave on them the names of the sons of Israel in the order of their birth – six names on one stone and the remaining six on the other. Engrave the names of the sons of Israel on the two stones the way a gem cutter engraves a seal. Then mount the stones in gold filigree settings and fasten them on the shoulder pieces of the ephod as memorial stones for the sons of Israel. Aaron is to bear the names on his shoulders as a memorial before the LORD. Make gold filigree settings and two braided chains of pure gold, like a rope, and attach the chains to the settings.

---

40 www.templemountfaithful.org

The Breastpiece

Fashion a breastpiece for making decisions – the work of skilled hands. Make it like the ephod: of gold, and of blue, purple and scarlet yarn, and of finely twisted linen. It is to be square – a span long and a span wide – and folded double. Then mount four rows of precious stones on it. The first row shall be carnelian, chrysolite and beryl; the second row shall be turquoise, lapis lazuli and emerald; the third row shall be jacinth, agate and amethyst; the fourth row shall be topaz, onyx and jasper Mount them in gold filigree settings. There are to be twelve stones, one for each of the names of the sons of Israel, each engraved like a seal with the name of one of the twelve tribes.

For the breastpiece make braided chains of pure gold, like a rope. Make two gold rings for it and fasten them to two corners of the breastpiece. Fasten the two gold chains to the rings at the corners of the breastpiece, and the other ends of the chains to the two settings, attaching them to the shoulder pieces of the ephod at the front. Make two gold rings and attach them to the other two corners of the breastpiece on the inside edge next to the ephod. Make two more gold rings and attach them to the bottom of the shoulder pieces on the front of the ephod, close to the seam just above the waistband of the ephod. The rings of the breastpiece are to be tied to the rings of the ephod with blue cord, connecting it to the waistband, so that the breastpiece will not swing out from the ephod.

A Jewish High Priest.

Whenever Aaron enters the Holy Place, he will bear the names of the sons of Israel over his heart on the breastpiece of decision as a continuing memorial before the LORD. Also put the Urim and the Thummim in the breastpiece, so they may be over Aaron's heart whenever he enters the presence of the LORD. Thus Aaron will always bear the means of making decisions for the Israelites over his heart before the LORD.

Other Priestly Garments

Make the robe of the ephod entirely of blue cloth, with an opening for the head in its centre. There shall be a woven edge like a collar around this opening, so that it will not tear. Make pomegranates of blue, purple and scarlet yarn around the hem of the robe, with gold bells between them. The gold bells and the pomegranates are to alternate around the hem of the robe. Aaron must wear it when he ministers. The sound of the bells will be heard when he enters the Holy Place before the

LORD and when he comes out, so that he will not die.

Make a plate of pure gold and engrave on it as on a seal: HOLY TO THE LORD. Fasten a blue cord to it to attach it to the turban; it is to be on the front of the turban. It will be on Aaron's forehead, and he will bear the guilt involved in the sacred gifts the Israelites consecrate, whatever their gifts may be. It will be on Aaron's forehead continually so that they will be acceptable to the LORD.

Weave the tunic of fine linen and make the turban of fine linen. The sash is to be the work of an embroiderer. Make tunics, sashes and caps for Aaron's sons to give them dignity and honor. After you put these clothes on your brother Aaron and his sons, anoint and ordain them. Consecrate them so they may serve me as priests.

Make linen undergarments as a covering for the body, reaching from the waist to the thigh. Aaron and his sons must wear them whenever they enter the tent of meeting or approach the altar to minister in the Holy Place, so that they will not incur guilt and die.

This is to be a lasting ordinance for Aaron and his descendants.

We will return to the High Priest's garments when looking at the Installation of the Third Principal, Joshua.

The Duties of the Three Principals of a Chapter

We have seen what the Three Principals represent symbolically and we have looked at the jewels they wear; we now need to look at their roles in our Chapters.

Zerubbabel, as the ritual says, occupies '*The highest honour the Chapter can confer*' and should therefore be '*to all men and especially to Masons an example of that moral rectitude of conduct which alone can entitle him to the goodwill and affection of the Companions and the respect and homage due to the office*'. Up until recently, the Z of a Chapter will, of necessity, have been a Craft Past Master of at least three years' experience. Since 2004 this has no longer been the case (although I haven't come across anyone reaching even the Third Principal's chair without being a Past Master because, whilst I'm sure some have, the practical side of it is that most Masons are too busy in their Craft lodges to do a lot in Chapter before they go through the Craft chair). In other jurisdictions, notably the Scottish, this stricture never applied because there the Craft and Royal Arch are entirely separate.

Z's duties are both ceremonial and administrative. He is not the sole ruler but *primus inter pares* (first among equals) and, as such, should always be prepared to consult his fellow Principals, be it on a ceremonial matter or some point regarding the governance of the Chapter. It is a responsible role and obviously the first requirement is attendance. It helps if he is a good ritualist because the ceremony of Exaltation is largely between Z and the Principal Sojourner. He may be part of a 'rule of three' but the Charter of the Chapter is delivered to him alone at the Installation, he has the right to preside at all convocations and has a casting vote in the event of a tie. He has a duty to enforce the by-laws of the Chapter and will, of course, automatically become Immediate Past Zerubbabel when his term of office ends.

The Second Principal, H, fulfils the obvious duties of assisting in the ceremony (particularly when he is asked by Z to assist in communicating the secrets). In addition to that he has to prepare himself to succeed to the First Chair by mastering the ceremony and deciding who is right for progression in his year and who is not.

J, as Third Principal, does not now have to be an Installed Master in the Craft and so this may be his first taste of Masonic rulership. He is not being 'thrown in at the deep end' to a great extent because his part in the ceremony is reasonably small but obviously he needs to be thoroughly conversant with the openings and closings and have an eye to the future by a close observation of the next two chairs which he will hopefully succeed to.

All three Principals should endeavour to deliver the lecture appropriate to their chair at least once during their term of office. My own experience is that J does the Historical Lecture, H the Symbolical Lecture and Z the Mystical Lecture. The Explanation of the Signs is now separated from the rest of the Mystical Lecture in some rituals and Z may feel it politic to get a Past Z to do this. The Signs and the Mystical Lecture should always be given on an evening when a candidate is exalted. One other lecture can possibly also be fitted in. Some Chapters do all three in the same evening after exalting a candidate. With the greatest possible respect, I think this is a bit 'heavy'.

CHAPTER 5
The Scribes

The Book of Nehemiah chapter 8 vv1–18 (Authorized version) tells us this:

And all the people gathered themselves together as one man into the street that was before the water gate; and they spake unto Ezra the scribe to bring the book of the law of Moses, which the LORD had commanded to Israel.

And Ezra the priest brought the law before the congregation both of men and women, and all that could hear with understanding, upon the first day of the seventh month.

And he read therein before the street that was before the water gate from the morning until midday, before the men and the women, and those that could understand; and the ears of all the people were attentive unto the book of the law.

And Ezra the scribe stood upon a pulpit of wood, which they had made for the purpose; and beside him stood Mattithiah, and Shema, and Anaiah, and Urijah, and Hilkiah, and Maaseiah, on his right hand; and on his left hand, Pedaiah, and Mishael, and Malchiah, and Hashum, and Hashbadana, Zechariah, and Meshullam.

An ancient Hebrew scribe.

And Ezra opened the book in the sight of all the people; (for he was above all the people;) and when he opened it, all the people stood up:

And Ezra blessed the LORD, the great God. And all the people answered, Amen, Amen, with lifting up their hands: and they bowed their heads, and worshipped the LORD with their faces to the ground.

Also Jeshua, and Bani, and Sherebiah, Jamin, Akkub, Shabbethai, Hodijah, Maaseiah, Kelita, Azariah, Jozabad, Hanan, Pelaiah, and the Levites, caused the people to understand the law: and the people stood in their place.

So they read in the book in the law of God distinctly, and gave the sense, and caused them to understand the reading.

And Nehemiah, which is the Tirshatha, and Ezra the priest the scribe, and the Levites that taught the people, said unto all the people, This day is holy unto the LORD your God; mourn not, nor weep. For all the people wept, when they heard the words of the law.

Then he said unto them, Go your way, eat the fat, and drink the sweet, and send portions unto them for whom nothing is prepared: for this day is holy unto our LORD: neither be ye sorry; for the joy of the LORD is your strength.

So the Levites stilled all the people, saying, Hold your peace, for the day is holy; neither be ye grieved.

And all the people went their way to eat, and to drink, and to send portions, and to make great mirth, because they had understood the words that were declared unto them.

And on the second day were gathered together the chief of the fathers of all the people, the priests, and the Levites, unto Ezra the scribe, even to understand the words of the law.

And they found written in the law which the LORD had commanded by Moses, that the children of Israel should dwell in booths in the feast of the seventh month:

And that they should publish and proclaim in all their cities, and in Jerusalem, saying, Go forth unto the mount, and fetch olive branches, and pine branches, and myrtle branches, and palm branches, and branches of thick trees, to make booths, as it is written.

So the people went forth, and brought them, and made themselves booths, every one upon the roof of his house, and in their courts, and in the courts of the house of God, and in the street of the water gate, and in the street of the gate of Ephraim.

And all the congregation of them that were come again out of the captivity made booths, and sat under the booths: for since the days of Jeshua the son of Nun unto that day had not the children of Israel done so. And there was very great gladness.

Also day by day, from the first day unto the last day, he read in the book of the law of God. And they kept the feast seven days; and on the eighth day was a solemn assembly, according unto the manner.

There are one or two points in need of clarification here. Firstly what is happening is in accordance with the reading selected for the Installation of a Second Principal (see Chapter 10) from the 1 Samuel chapter 3: *And the word of the LORD was precious in those days; there was no open vision.* In other words the ordinary people did not have access to the scriptures, the law of Moses. Ezra is the 'lector and expounder', reading and explaining the scriptures, for which the people are suitably grateful. The word '*Tirshatha*' means governor and is the title accorded to a Provincial Grand Master in the Royal Order of Scotland. Finally what is being celebrated is the Jewish Feast of the Tabernacles, otherwise known as the Feast of Booths or Sukkot. This was not the first time Sukkot had been celebrated, in fact King Solomon dedicated the First Temple during the period of Sukkot which normally occurs in the month of Tishrei (late September or early October), but it was the first time it had been celebrated since the return from the Babylonish captivity. During this feast some Jews build booths in which they live, eat and sleep during the seven-day feast which is followed by Simchat Torah or Rejoicing in the Law.

The names Ezra and Nehemiah are synonymous with Royal Arch Masonry but their origins and the people who originally bore those names are perhaps not so well known.

To look at Ezra first and to estimate the contribution he made to the life of his people it is necessary that we should understand a little of how the Jewish faith works. Central to everything in Judaism is law. That is the definitive characteristic of Judaism, which sets it apart from any other religion.

That law is contained in the most sacred of Jewish texts – the Torah – which consists of the first five books of the Old Testament – the Pentateuch: Genesis, Exodus, Leviticus, Numbers and Deuteronomy.

This of itself says much of the nature of our Royal Arch ceremony. The Sojourners find the sacred Torah but it is dismissed as nothing more than 'a scroll of vellum or parchment'. What is found on the second attempt – the Sacred and Mysterious name, the genuine secret of Masonry – is given much more pre-eminence.

Now, we already know the truth of the matter. Hiram Abif was not murdered by three ruffians. That is only a legend allowing us to lose secrets in the Craft and find them in the Royal Arch.

But the scroll, or more correctly the Torah, was lost. And it was found!

In Irish Royal Arch masonry the scroll is the treasure which is rediscovered – the Law of Moses as handed down by God Himself on Mount Sinai.

Of course, this treasure was not in the form of the original tables of stone. They, along with the pot of manna, the shewbread, Aaron's Rod and the Ark of the Covenant which had contained them and also the sacred fire and the Urim and Thummim (see Chapter 13) were gone. They all disappeared at the destruction of Solomon's Temple.

The other sacred text of Judaism is the Talmud. As the Torah is described as the cornerstone, the Talmud is seen as the central pillar of Judaism. It is in two parts – the Mishnah, which is a summary of the tradition of oral law which has grown up around the written law of the Torah, and the Gemarah which is a commentary on the Mishnah.

What has this to do with Ezra? Well, although in the First Temple era there were what were called *Tofsei Torah* – people learned in the Law of Moses – it was at the time of the Second Temple that we see the emergence of scribes as such whose function it was to interpret the laws contained in the Torah, as we saw in the scripture reading above. In the New Testament we hear of Jesus being heckled by the Scribes and Pharisees. If you have ever wondered what the scribes did – what they wrote – their function was interpretation and teaching in the same way that Ezra did.

Ezra the Scribe would read to the people from the Torah and a group of Levites would expound on the doctrines therein contained. Remember the tribe of Levi were being punished by God for their part, with the tribe of Simeon, in the barbarous murder of the Shechamites. They were accordingly given no land of their own and were devoted exclusively to the service of the altar.

In Ezekiel 7:6 we are told that Ezra was *'a ready scribe in the law of Moses which the Lord God of Israel had given'*. In Ezra's own book at chapter 7 verse 10 it says *'For Ezra had prepared his heart to seek the law of the Lord and to do it and to teach in Israel statutes and judgement'*. He was also the precursor and founder of the *Knesset Gedolah* or Great Assembly who between 520 BC and AD 70 canonised, or edited, the Bible, deciding which books and which chapters of which books should be included or omitted.

Ezra, then, could be fairly described as an ecclesiastical lawyer, but the importance of this should not be underestimated, given the total preoccupation of the Jewish religion with law. In the apocryphal book of Esdras at chapter 9 it says:

So Esdras the chief priest brought the law unto the whole multitude from man to woman, and to all the priests, to hear law in the first day of the seventh month. And he read in the broad court before the holy porch from morning unto midday, before both men and women; and the multitude gave heed unto the law. And Esdras the priest and reader of the law stood up upon a pulpit of wood, which was made for that purpose.

Esdras, by the way, is the Greek spelling of Ezra.

The other thing we got from Ezra is worship. Quite simply that; systematic, what today we would call liturgical, worship. Before Ezra's time we hear of people praising God but this would tend to be spontaneous, thanking Him for deliverance from something or other or beseeching Him to grant some prayer or other. Either of these might be accompanied by the sacrifice of one or more animals. The idea of attending at a fixed place and worshipping according to a given form of words was hitherto unknown.

In around 538 BC, forty-two thousand of the Children of Israel returned from captivity in Babylon (although modern scholarship considers this to be an exaggeration because it is thought that nowhere near that number actually returned). Ezra was not amongst them. In fact he wasn't even born. The Second Temple was not completed during the reign of Cyrus, King of Persia because efforts to build it were frustrated by the enemies of Israel. It was finished in the reign of King Darius but we are also told that it later fell into disrepair, so much so that if you go to Jerusalem today your guide will tell you that there were only two temples

– King Solomon's and the one built by Herod the Great which we are told in the Historical Lecture was destroyed by the Romans under Titus in the year AD 70. Herod in fact restored the building, which Zerubbabel and Co. had begun.

Ezra was the great-grandson of the prophet Hilkiah (whom we encounter in the Irish version of the legend – see Chapter 12) and a direct descendant of Aaron, the brother of Moses. We understand he returned from Babylon in about the year 458 BC (a long time after the building of the Second Temple) during the reign of King Ataxerxes. It is not therefore possible for him to have conversed with Zerubbabel as our ceremony would have us believe.

As an aside I may also add that it is unlikely that even Zerubbabel was in at the dedication of the Second Temple, because he seems to have faded off the scene before the rebuilding was complete.

What then was Ezra's role in coming to Jerusalem if it wasn't to take part in the rebuilding of the Temple? Have you ever wondered why the Persian Kings would wish to help out in the rebuilding of the Jewish Temple? Why should they be bothered? As you would expect, the answer is political. The Persians were in the business of empire-building and in those days they were prepared to practise tolerance in order to preserve equilibrium within their empire.

By the time of Ataxerxes the plot had thickened. The Athenians, under Pericles, had come to the aid of a group in Egypt who were fomenting revolt against the Persian Empire. Ataxerxes' motive was to ensure the loyalty of his Jewish subjects and he sent Ezra to Jerusalem to ensure that the true Jewish law – the law of the Torah – was being enforced. In other words he was buying their compliance.

Ezra found that all was not well. Since the return from captivity there had been intermarriage outside the faith and this was forbidden because it might lead to the worship of foreign Gods. He therefore ordered that all foreign wives and their children were to be repudiated.

Turning now to Nehemiah (the son of Hechaliah and probably of the Tribe of Judah), there is some debate as to whether or not he and Ezra were contemporaries. It is possible they were – Ezra is mentioned in the Book of Nehemiah – and that their paths crossed. It is not a fact that they were *'Attendants on the Grand Sanhedrin'* at one and the same time – if at all. Indeed it is probably wrong to refer to Nehemiah as a scribe, in the sense we have defined it, at all, any more than he is in a Royal Arch Chapter where he actually performs the function of an Inner Guard.

In Babylon Nehemiah held the office of Cupbearer to King Ataxerxes. He also acted for the Persian Queen in some capacity and was probably a eunuch. The express reason for his return to Jerusalem was to rebuild the walls of the city.

Ataxerxes knew what he was doing because a serious revolt had broken out in Egypt and there was a need for increased security in the southern part of his empire.

In Jerusalem, Nehemiah was the object of a piece of trickery when a character called Shamaiah tried to lure him into the sanctuary of the Temple, a place where eunuchs were forbidden to enter. According to the Torah, *no one whose testicles are crushed or whose penis is cut off shall be admitted to the assembly of the Lord.* There is some dispute about this because of translation from the original Hebrew and Greek. It may have been because Nehemiah was not a priest that he was forbidden to go into the most holy places.

We should note that Nehemiah's journey to Jerusalem involved a political role, whereas Ezra's had been religious.

Nehemiah went there to rebuild the wall and provide a defence against enemy attack, having the status of Governor of Judah (or Tirshatha) and escorted by a substantial military force.

Torah Scrolls today.

We are told in the Book of Nehemiah that the wall was rebuilt in fifty-two days. That seems quick but the pressure was on. Jerusalem was encircled by enemies in the form of Philistines, Arabs, Samaritans and Ammonites any one of whom could have attacked at any time. It is worth remembering that the Athenians got a wall round Athens in a month under similar circumstances and, under the threat of attack by Attila the Hun, the Romans put one round Constantinople in sixty days.

Nehemiah's wall ran from the Sheep Gate in the north, to the Hananel Tower at the north west corner, the Fish Gate in the west, the Furnaces Tower at the Temple Mount's south west corner, the Dung Gate in the south, the East Gate and the gate beneath the Golden Gate in the east.

The following doggerel verse appears in the ritual of the Royal Order of Scotland:

When Sanballat Jerusalem distressed
With sharp assaults in Nehemiah's time,

The Jews themselves for war or work addressed,
And did repair their walls with stone and lime.
One hand the sword against the foe did shake,
The other hand the trowel up did take.
Oh! Valiant minds, lo! here's a worthy part,
The Jews quailed not at the ruin of their wall,
But, champion-like, improved Freemason's Art;
Which does infer this lesson to us all,
That, to defend our country dear from harm,
For war or work we either hand should arm.[41]

Now, I doubt if even many members of the Royal Order will know anything about Sanballat so, as the incident is relevant to Nehemiah, I will try and fill in the gaps. First of all who was Sanballat?

When Governor Nehemiah returned to Jerusalem with his armed escort to rebuild the walls the people who were already there (Samaritans and Philistines) laughed him to scorn. Sanballat was the ruler of the Samaritans and he along with some of the remnant of the Jews living in Jerusalem (presumably 'that menial tribe left behind by the Babylonish general for the purpose of tilling the land') tried to stop him doing it by attacking Nehemiah's workmen. This is the reason they had 'a trowel in one hand and a sword by their side', as we see in the verse above and also in the Symbolical Lecture.

Nehemiah held sway as Governor of Judah for twelve years. One of his primary responsibilities was of course to collect taxes, in spite of which he seems to have been popular because he had regard for his people and collected nothing for the maintenance of his own household. At one time when it was clear that the Jews were struggling to meet the tithes for the Persian Court and the upkeep of their own Temple, Nehemiah cancelled all debts to avert widespread bankruptcy.

He then took measures to repopulate the city and purify the Jewish community, enforcing the cancellation of debt, assisting Ezra to promulgate the Law of Moses, and enforcing the divorce of Jewish men from their non-Jewish wives.

At the end of this twelve-year stint, Nehemiah returned to Persia. He came back to Jerusalem a few years later to find that the principles of good government he had laid down were being neglected. An unscrupulous person called Tobias the Ammonite had occupied the Temple, the

---

41 The Official Ritual of the Rosy Cross – published in Edinburgh by the Royal Order of Scotland

The 'Ark' in a modern synagogue – effectively a bookcase – in which the Sacred Scrolls are kept.

Sabbath was being desecrated by foreign traders and the inter-marriage thing had started again. Nehemiah responded to this violently by throwing Tobias' furniture out of the Temple and then physically assaulting some offenders and pulling out their hair!

One thing Nehemiah did do in connection with the Temple was to organise a search for the Sacred Fire, which had been lost. Digging down they came upon – not fire – but what they described as 'thick water', which according to the Book of Maccabees, when ignited 'kindled a great blaze so that all men marveled'. It is a wonder they were still around to marvel because what they had discovered, which they called naphtha, was of course a crude form of petrol.

Nothing whatsoever is known about the end of Ezra or Nehemiah. They did not write the books of the Bible which bear their names. That was probably done by a team – the same one that wrote the Book of Chronicles. Of the reasons for the decision of our forebears to use their names to describe the functions of secretary and inner guard, nothing is known either – I suppose they had to call them something!

Modern Functions

The two scribes are key officers of any Royal Arch Chapter and their importance cannot be understated. They have both an administrative and a ritualistic function. Ezra will usually be a Past First Principal, unless he is the sort of chap who likes to concentrate on administrative work, rather than progressing through the several chairs. He will still have to be a bit of a ritualist though. His duties will include (and I say 'include' because local conditions vary) summoning convocations, keeping minutes and membership records, dealing with correspondence, keeping the Principals (and anyone else who needs to know) aware of developments in Grand Chapter as well as in the Province or District, informing the Almoner of cases of sickness or distress, booking meals and making other arrangements for the festive board etc., etc.

Ezra's ritual function is firstly to supply the Sojourners and candidate with the proper working implements, then to check the report of the Principal Sojourner as to his discovery and to report to the Principals after which the Scribes will be instructed to divest the workmen of the instruments of labour and finally to instruct them to advance to the east for a further reward.

Nehemiah will often be something of a 'rising star'. Often he will have performed the role of Principal Sojourner and thus proved his ritual prowess. Now he is waiting to succeed to the Principals' chairs. This gives him a good chance for a look round and to observe the Principals and their roles so that he will be ready when his turn comes (and Chapter years with fewer meetings than the Craft tend to pass even more quickly!).

Ritually he assists Ezra in the duties outlined above but of course he also has to be the Inner Guard, announcing candidates, members and visitors. This is his greatest speaking part.

Both Ezra and Nehemiah are usually members of the Chapter Committee because their roles are of sufficient importance to allow them a participation in the running of the Chapter.

At Provincial level, it was often our custom in the Province of Cheshire to appoint a clergyman to the position of Provincial Grand Scribe Nehemiah, who would thereafter succeed to the priestly function of Third Provincial Grand Principal.

CHAPTER 6
The Sojourners

Now this doctrine, that labour is worship, is the very doctrine that have been advanced and maintained, from time immemorial, as a leading dogma of the Order of Freemasonry. There is no other human institution under the sun which have set forth this great principle in such bold relief. We hear constantly of Freemasonry as an institution that inculcates morality, that fosters the social feeling, that teaches brotherly love, and all this is well, because it is true; but we must never forget that from its foundation-stone to its pinnacle, all over its vast temple, is inscribed, in symbols of living light, the great truth that labour is worship.

Albert G. Mackey, The Symbolism of Freemasonry *(1882)*

The dictionary defines a 'Sojourner' as one who stays temporarily. This is in a way curious because it implies, in our case, that the three men who present themselves before the Grand Sanhedrin, having travelled all the way from Babylon have only come back to Jerusalem to help rebuild the Temple on a sort of 'job and finish' basis, after which they would return to whence they came. Having been released from their captivity by King Cyrus of Persia, would they not wish to rebuild the Temple and then remain in their native land? The true derivation of the word is 'day-labourer' which fits our purpose but it could also be argued that they were sojourning in Babylon and had now come home to take part in the work of rebuilding.

In the Ceremony of Passing of the Veils (in some versions of it anyway) these three men are actually named as we will see in Chapter 11.

For our purposes, in normal English Constitution working, they are three members of the Chapter who have come to work on a building site. The Principal Sojourner has the speaking part in the Royal Arch drama and is helped out by a First Assistant Sojourner and a Second Assistant Sojourner, who do not speak. The last of these does not have a lot to do and the office provides a useful first step on the ladder for aspiring

*Collar Jewel of
Principal Sojourner.*

Companions. Effectively, when the candidate comes in, the Second Assistant Sojourner is redundant except in certain rituals where he and the First Assistant unveil the altar and also in rituals where the nine officers are called to explain their duties when he replies:

'At the left of the Principal Sojourner and, in conjunction with the 1st Assistant Sojourner, to aid and assist him in his duties, Most Excellent.'

The First Assistant Sojourner is still a non-speaking part but he has quite a bit to do and needs to be on the ball. His duties are similarly described.

When the Principal Sojourner is asked for his situation and duty, he replies: '*In the west, Most Excellent, to examine candidates and afterwards to prepare them for and conduct them through the ceremony of Exaltation.*'

In another version of the Opening Ceremony, the Principal Sojourner states his duty as '*To introduce all Sojourners from the Babylonish captivity and such as are able to do the Lord's work at this grand offering of peace; to report all discoveries that may come to my present knowledge.*'

This is rather understating matters because the Principal Sojourner can make or break the ceremony. A Companion who is competent in that role will have studied the Royal Arch and mastered the two longest pieces of ritual involved. It is quite common for Chapters, particularly those who may be a bit short-handed (or lacking in candidates), to rely on a Companion who is very experienced to fill that role on a sort of semi-permanent basis, even though that Companion may well be a PZ or even a Grand or Provincial Officer. This practice is not really to be encouraged and the better way to do it is to split the Principal Sojourner's work between him and his two assistants.

The most common thing said about the job of Principal Sojourner by those who have done it is 'I could do it for ever,' because it is a very satisfying role which basically involves telling two longish stories. And, as we all know, stories are the easiest form of ritual to learn.

In former times the Sojourners were known as the Principal Sojourner, the Senior Sojourner and the Junior Sojourner. In some versions of the Passing of the Veils, they acted as Captains of the veils. In others they guided the candidates through the veils and other officers were appointed as Captains of those veils as is still the case in Scotland and Ireland (see Appendix 3 and Appendix 4).

But, outwith that, Sojourners have been around from the very earliest days and always had a key role to play in the presentation of the Royal Arch drama. The first Grand Chapter, established in 1766, provided for Sojourners to be elected annually and eventually some Chapters gave power to the Principal Sojourner to appoint his assistants. Bernard Jones points out that a provision to that effect was contained in the RA regulations of 1823 and was only removed in 1886 when the power of appointment of officers was vested in the Chapter.[42] Officers were all once elected annually but it is possible to resolve that the Three Principals be empowered to appoint all officers other than the Treasurer and the Janitor – this of course being in line with Craft practice.

Collar Jewel of Assistant Sojourner.

---

42 Bernard E. Jones – *Freemasons' Royal Arch Guide*

But let's just consider for a moment what the Sojourners actually do. They dig down in the ruins of the First Temple and, first of all find the sacred writings, and then go on to find a block of white marble with the names, or rather initials, of the Three Grand Masters engraved on the front. On top of the pedestal they find a plate of gold with a circle and triangle in which is contained the true name of God. What they have found cannot be new intelligence to the Three Principals, to whom that name must have been transmitted. Nor can it be anything new to Ezra and Nehemiah because otherwise they would not be able to state, after going to the spot to inspect the discovery: '*Correct, Most Excellent, in every particular*'. Now we know that this is legend, as opposed to fact but, to develop that legend a little more, the Lecture in the Degree of Royal Master in the Order of Royal and Select Masters says this:

Following the death of our Grand Master Hiram Abif it was at first supposed that the Master Word had been lost. Having been informed by Adoniram that it was Hiram Abif's wish that, in the event of his death, the Master Word should be deposited beneath the Sanctum Sanctorum or Holy of Holies of the Temple, our two remaining Grand Masters agreed to deposit it in the ninth arch of the Secret Vault, on top of the Ark of the Covenant, in a triangular form and in three languages, Syrian, Chaldean and Egyptian, so that if the Children of Israel should ever be carried into captivity and remain for so long as to forget their mother tongue, yet on their return, if found, it might be restored by means of the other languages.

And that it might be known and distinguished as the Master Word, they placed on top of the Ark of the Covenant the three Grand Masters' jewels, inscribed one in each language, knowing that the descriptions thereof would be handed down to the latest posterity.[43]

This, presumably, is how the Principals and the Scribes would have already been aware of what the Sojourners were about to find.

---

43 Ritual of the Order of Royal and Select Masters

CHAPTER 7

The Other Officers of a
Royal Arch Chapter

The principal offices having already been filled, as we say in the ritual, let us look at the functions of the other 'players' in a Royal Arch Chapter. Unless they are standing in, as is often necessary, for a missing Companion, they have no ritual function and so their activities need not detain us long, but their functions nonetheless help to ensure the Chapter's smooth running.

The Treasurer

As in every Masonic unit, the role of the Treasurer is pivotal in seeing that we remain solvent. He collects members' subscriptions, as well as fees for Exaltation and joining and pays out dues to Grand Chapter and to Provincial or District Grand Chapter, where applicable. He is bound to maintain a bank account and to produce annual accounts for both the Chapter General Fund and, in conjunction with the Almoner and Charity Steward, the Alms Fund. His jewel is a key, as in the Craft and with the same symbolism but, as with all Royal Arch officers' collar jewels, set within a triangle.

Collar Jewel of Treasurer.

The Director of Ceremonies

DCs often have to put up with a lot of flak and take much criticism but their role in the Royal Arch really is key. A RA Chapter has a lot more equipment than is usual in the Craft, Mark or other Orders and his knowledge of how the Chapter should be set out has to be good. Unless you have a room in your Masonic Hall permanently set out for Chapter (as in Liverpool – see above), it is likely that the DC will have to start from a bare room and lay everything out in its proper place. In this of course he should be assisted by the ADC and other Companions because it is a big job. Equally, breaking down the Chapter after a convocation needs assistance not just in removing the items but also making sure that they are properly stowed away to be found easily when laying out for the next time the Chapter meets. In addition to this there is the usual pressure of covering offices when Companions are unable to attend to ensure that the candidate gets the best ceremony of Exaltation that he can be given. Because the DC is responsible for presenting the Principals Elect at the Installation, it is highly recommended that he be a PZ – he

Collar Jewel of Director of Ceremonies.

really needs to be to appreciate the 'big picture'. His jewel is crossed wands within a triangle.

Collar Jewel of Charity Steward.

The Charity Steward

Charity may often be considered of less importance in the Royal Arch than in the Craft, especially when Companions are already making charitable contributions in their Craft lodges but this should not really be the case. A Chapter may well comprise brethren from a number of lodges and the Charity Steward should identify suitable destinations at national, regional and local level for their charitable giving. As a well-known grocer says 'Every little helps' and the Charity Steward should encourage additional contributions where possible. The jewel of the office is a trowel within a triangle.

Collar Jewel of Almoner.

The Almoner

Similarly, because of the different lodge background of some of the Companions the role of the Almoner is important because in cases of sickness or distress, the more visits or phone calls a companion receives to show that people care about him the better. Again, it should not be left to the Craft lodge alone to perform this function. The Almoner should report cases of sickness and distress at every convocation and suggest to the Charity Steward and the companions suitable objects for donations. His jewel is a purse within a triangle.

Collar Jewel of Assistant Scribe E.

The Assistant Scribe E

I am currently Scribe E of two Chapters and I believe that there can be plenty for an Assistant Scribe E to do. In these days of email the distribution of summonses has become much easier and printing costs are much reduced, so that use of the Assistant Secretary/Scribe E is probably no longer necessary, but the Assistant Scribe E could for example take the minutes of committee meetings and assist in the collection of dining fees. It very much depends on local circumstances, but it seems only fair not to burden your Scribe E and Treasurer too much – remember they are mortal, have families and probably have many other Masonic commitments as well. The jewel is crossed pens within a triangle with the word 'ASSISTANT'.

Collar Jewel of Assistant Director of Ceremonies.

The Assistant Director of Ceremonies

Given the considerable duties of the DC as outlined above, the services of an assistant can prove very useful. He does not have to be a PZ (although it probably helps if he is) but his early attendance and help with laying out and breaking down are very important. His jewel is crossed wands within a triangle with the word 'ASSISTANT'.

The Organist

The role of the Organist may be fairly self-explanatory but there is no doubt that music makes a difference. Even if it is only for incoming and outgoing processions and opening and closing odes, the addition of music really enhances the proceedings. If you have not got an Organist (and they are like hens' teeth nowadays), consider music on a CD. Your 'Organist' then only needs to know how to operate the machine. Real live organists should try to keep their repertoire up to date and to keep adding new marches and incidental music. The jewel is a lyre within a triangle.

Collar Jewel of Organist.

The Stewards

Being a Steward in a Chapter is a chance to 'look round'. The ceremonies will be unfamiliar to you and take a bit of getting used to. But do not just pour the wine at the dinner table. Look, listen and learn and when you feel reasonably confident, volunteer to act as an Assistant Sojourner and start reading and learning the Sojourners' work. That is how you 'get into' the Royal Arch, make progress and get more enjoyment out of your Chapter membership. The jewel is a cornucopia or horn of plenty within a triangle.

Collar Jewel of Steward.

The Janitor

It seems unfair to cover the Janitor last because, as we have seen, he is one of the nine principal officers of the Chapter. Janitors were formerly known as Tylers. The name is derived from the Roman god Janus and from the Latin for an entrance or a key – thus January, the gate of the year. The word used to be in common use to mean a caretaker or porter.[44]

Collar Jewel of Janitor.

The Janitor's task, like a Tyler's, is one of initial preparation of candidates and then acting as doorkeeper. There are three occasions on which he will knock at the door (other than to announce guests or late arrivals) and he should know the correct knocks to use as shown in the ritual. He will normally be involved also in setting up and breaking down the Chapter – BUT HE SHOULDN'T BE LEFT TO DO IT ON HIS OWN!

---

44 Frederick Smyth – *A Reference Book for Freemasons*

CHAPTER 8

The Ceremony of Exaltation

Background

We cannot know what the original ceremony of Exaltation into Royal Arch Masonry was like. We know that at one time it was part of the Third Degree of the Craft. Just as these days we are encouraged to split up the work, e.g. the giving of Charges, the Tracing Board explanations, the tools, the Third Degree history and the Royal Arch lectures, we know that much ritual in the 18th century was given sitting round a table in catechetical form. This method of doing things is said to have been derived from the Rosicrucians.

We also know that there were certain expert Masons who were recognised and appointed to discharge the Lectures or explanation of the history and symbolism lying behind the ceremonies performed. In the North of England (particularly in County Durham) this developed into travelling teams of such overseers called Harodim or Highroadim, who would visit a centre at which Masons would assemble to receive this further instruction in the five degrees of Craft, Royal Arch and Knights Templar. In the 19th century a similar practice was adopted in the same area of England to instruct Mark Masons in the meaning of the ancient forms and practices of that degree.[45] Some writers have confused the Degree of Harodim with that of Passed Master, which was a device contrived to enable brethren who were not Past Masters to join the Royal Arch. This is not necessarily true – Harodim was a different matter altogether and rather resembled the Irish Lodge of Instruction (see chapter 2). The name Harodim derives from the overseers appointed to supervise the work at King Solomon's Temple. As we read in 1 Kings 5:16:

Beside the chief of Solomon's officers which were over the work, three thousand and three hundred, which ruled over the people that wrought in the work.

The Book of Chronicles differs in the number of these overseers at 2 Chronicles 2:2 and 18:

And Solomon told out threescore and ten thousand men to bear burdens, and fourscore thousand to hew in the mountain, and three thousand and six hundred to oversee them. And he set threescore and ten thousand of them to be bearers of burdens, and fourscore thousand to be hewers in the mountain, and three thousand and six hundred overseers to set the people a work.

The records of Palatine Lodge No.17 in the Province of Durham

---

45 Bro Rev Neville Barker Cryer – lecture given at Internet Lodge No. 9659, 13 October 2001

show that, in the 18th century, Degrees called Passed Master, Passing the Bridge and Harodim were worked. Passed Master we know about. Passing the Bridge seems to have been a precursor to the Royal Arch and from extant knowledge of the Allied Degree of Red Cross of Babylon and Irish Knight Masonry, we may presume a connection to the journey of the returning Israelites after Cyrus had allowed them to return to their own country.

William Preston says of the Harodim:

A degree very popular in the north of England, especially in the county of Durham, and probably founded in 1681. It was brought under the Grand Lodge in 1735. Members were the custodians of the Ritual of All Masonry, or the Old York Ritual. There were nine lodges in all. A London version of this society was the Harodim-Rosy-Cross, – probably carried to London by the earl of Derwentwater. In 1787 a Grand Chapter of the Ancient and Venerable Order of Harodim was founded by William Preston, author of Illustrations of Masonry (1775).[46]

It would appear that the Degree of Harodim had disappeared by 1811 and, following the Union, that scion of the Emulation Lodge of Improvement, Peter Gilkes, came up to Durham and introduced the new Craft Degrees. Nonetheless we owe a debt to the Harodim and to Palatine Lodge, as well as the celebrated lodge at Swalwell, for encouraging ritual purity in the Royal Arch and elsewhere.

The Opening of the Chapter

We might begin by asking what is a Chapter? One ritual, written by the late Cyril Batham, begins with the First Principal asking 'In what place are we?' The Principal Sojourner answers 'We are in the centre of the Most Sacred Place on Earth.'

That, when you think about it, accurately sums up the location of the Three Original Grand Lodges. Certainly they were sacred to the Jews but even to others likewise because God actually dwelt in the Tabernacle in the wilderness and in King Solomon's Temple. In the case of the Temple we are concerned with in the Royal Arch, He had pledged that He was still with His people.

Before we can exalt anyone we first have to open the Chapter and there are a number of important points about this. In the ritual of the Perfect Ceremonies[47] there are two methods of opening a RA Chapter: a private opening at which only the Three Principals and Past Principals would be present and a public opening in the presence of all RA Companions.

---

46 Preston, William. *Illustrations of Masonry*. London, 1775.
47 The Perfect Ceremonies of the Supreme Order of the Holy Royal Arch

Other rituals do not have this facility but it is nonetheless worth looking at.

The private opening consists of a long prayer, readings from the prophesies of Zechariah about the return of Zerubbabel and the rebuilding of God's House, sometimes a reading from Isaiah (at which book the VSL is opened) and the Chapter being opened in the true name of God. In the public version the long prayer is used at the end and the scripture reading is from Psalm 24 – *Lift up your heads, O ye gates etc.*

In the days when the Chapter ceremony was preceded by the Passing of the Veils (see chapter 11), this private ceremony of opening was in regular use. Principals and Past Principals would enter the Chapter and open it as above. The remaining Companions would then enter the Chapter in two columns, led by the Scribes Ezra and Nehemiah, and as many as possible would form into threes to prove themselves Royal Arch Masons in the way with which we are familiar. There sometimes followed the opening given in chapter 4 where the First Principal enquires of each of the officers as to their station and duties, like in a Craft lodge.

In the Royal Arch, as in all Masonry, we do things which we take for granted without understanding what they mean or where they came from. The Companions will stand to order to receive the Three Principals who will either come up to the east and then move to the west to start the opening, or they may just come in and stay in the west, depending on the custom of the Chapter. The first thing that happens after the Principals have taken their positions in the west is that they will advance by seven steps in sequence of three, then two, then a further two. This is a survival of the Veils ceremony, as is most of what happens at this point. After each group of steps the Principals bow and then a word is spoken. These words 'Omnipotent, Omniscient and Omnipresent' are attributes of the Deity and hence the bow before each one is spoken. Some rituals give them in the order shown and spoken by Z, then H, then J. Others give them in reverse order with J saying Omniscience and H saying Omnipresence (i.e. the noun rather than the adjective) but the end result is the same. The reasons for using these particular words are also connected with the Veils as we shall see in chapter 11 (but see also below).

Most rituals use the opening prayer (or a version of it):

Almighty God to whom all hearts are open, all desires known, and from whom no secrets are hid, cleanse the thoughts of our hearts by the inspiration of Thy Holy Spirit, that we may perfectly love Thee and worthily magnify Thy Holy Name.

This, as we saw above, will of course be known to many of us as the Collect said at the beginning of an Anglican Mass, although the words in church have now been modernised. A collect is something said when people have collected or gathered together, as we have gathered to open our Chapter.

Let us also look at a couple of other terms that we encounter for the first time when we join the Royal Arch.

The word 'Exaltation' means a raising in rank or power or to make lofty or noble. In Masonic terms this is a little confusing. We have already been raised when we received the Third Degree, in more than one sense of that word. Being made lofty or noble is hardly what the Royal Arch is about either.

We talk about the Royal Arch being a Supreme Degree. As Cryer points out that is because it was what it was originally intended to be – the *summum bonum* of all Freemasonry.[48] At one time it was referred to as the *sublime* degree but that subtitle is now accorded to the Third Degree of the Craft. We are after all revealing the true name of God here and that is about as 'supreme' as you can get. After the de-Christianisation of 1835, other degrees appeared which claimed to restore that which had been taken out.

There is also the fact that, when we join the Royal Arch, we become Companions. Now this is an interesting, if at times confusing, word. It is said to be derived from a word meaning people who eat bread together. Confusion arises because in France the word *Compagnon* means in Masonic terms a Fellowcraft. This derives from the titles of trade guilds or societies of journeymen in France, notably in the building trade. It has been said that the *Compagnonnage* influenced Freemasonry and from our point of view this makes sense because the apprentice (or aspirant) set to work in the First Degree on the rough ashlar graduates to become a fellow of the Craft or *compagnon* when he has completed to perfect ashlar in the Second Degree.

There are other meanings or connotations of the word. Wealthy people (usually elderly ladies) would employ a companion to help them when necessary and generally keep them company. In Cyprus and also in Crete we have a dialect word *kambare* used to mean 'mate'. It was originally an Italian word, derived from when the Venetians ruled those islands. If, outside Masonry, we described someone as an excellent companion we would be implying that it was a pleasure to be in his or her company.

In some professional organisations and societies the grade of Companion is the highest and implies complete mastery of whatever art or science that society practises. Conversely, in some orders of knighthood, Companion was the lowest grade and this, if you think about

---

48 Fraternity Chapter No.4072 – *Exaltation with Explanation* by Rev Neville Barker Cryer (2002)

it, is appropriate considering that – certainly under the Antients' Grand Lodge – the next place to go after the Royal Arch was the grade of Knight Templar where he is received as *'Companion so-and-so, a pilgrim on his travels, weary and fatigued'*. It is also worth bearing in mind that, whereas we do not share bread together in the Royal Arch, we do in the KT.

After the prayer, the Principals agree to keep their mysteries and then advance to the east by three, two and then two steps. The order in which they do this again depends on the ritual. Once in the east, they share the word, salute their sceptres and declare the Chapter open.

So let us look at the Exaltation Ceremony in detail. The Chapter is open and the early business of the Convocation (minutes etc.) has been disposed of. We are now ready to exalt our Masonic brother. At one time there had to be three candidates (representing the three Sojourners) but thankfully this is no longer the case in England and I have to say that the ceremony goes better when there is only one candidate. I once had to exalt two together (a father and son) at a time when my bottom dentures were in for repair – a hard night, that!

Preliminary Matters – the Preparation and Entrusting

So the first thing that will happen is the re-veiling of the altar, after which the Principal Sojourner is instructed to retire and entrust the candidate.

The pre-examination by the Principal Sojourner is straightforward enough. The candidate is being examined on his qualifications as a Master Mason. He is asked to confirm that he has been a Master Mason for four weeks and upwards.

At one time the Questions after Raising were put to a candidate for the Royal Arch. They are rarely heard in the Craft now, so are worth repeating here:

Q. *How got you raised to the S.D. of a M.M.?*
A. *By undergoing a previous examination in open L. and being entrusted with a test of merit leading to that degree.*
Q. *Where were you then conducted?*
A. *To a convenient room adjoining a M.M.'s L for the purpose of being ppd.*
Q. *How were you ppd?*
A. *By having ba's, bb's and bk's made b and bh's spd.*
Q. *What enabled you to gain admission?*
A. *The help of God, the united aid of the S & C's and the benefit of a PW.*
Q. *Which I will thank you to give.*
A. —   —   —

Q.	The import of the word?
A.	— — —
Q.	How did you gain admission?
A.	By the k's of F.C.
Q.	On what were you admitted?
A.	B.P's of the C's presented to b.b's.
Q.	On your admission to the L, did you observe anything different from its usual appearance?
A.	I did: all was d save for a g.l. in the E.
Q.	To what did that d allude?
A.	The d. of d.
Q.	Am I then to understand that d. is the peculiar subject if this Degree?
A.	It is indeed.
Q.	From what circumstance?
A.	The untimely d. of our M, HA.
Q.	What were the wt's with which our M was sl—n?
A.	The pr, l and h—y m—l.
Q.	How came you to be acquainted with his d.?
A.	By having figuratively represented our M, HA when I was raised to the d of a MM.
Q.	Were you raised and on what?
A.	I was; on the FP's of F.

In most Chapters, however, it is now simply a matter of the Principal Sojourner retiring to test the candidate and communicating to him what he needs to know.

We should look first at the preparation of the candidate. This is a lot less elaborate than it once was but why is the candidate hoodwinked?

The basic answer, as in the Craft, is 'so the heart might conceive before the eye may perceive'. Of course in the Craft if the candidate refuses to take his obligation he is led out of the lodge without seeing anything. The hoodwink has been described as '*a symbol of the secrecy, silence, and darkness in which the mysteries of our art should be preserved from the unhallowed gaze of the profane*'. It has been supposed to have a symbolic reference to the passage in St. John's Gospel (1:5), '*And the light shineth in darkness; and the darkness comprehended it not.*' It is more certain, however, that there is in the hoodwink a representation of the mystical darkness which always preceded the rites of the ancient initiations. But those of us who have passed through the ceremony of Exaltation will remember the wonderful sight we saw when the hoodwink was removed.

The manner of preparation of the candidate has changed over the years. At the beginning of the last century, he would be prepared as for the Third Degree and would then have a cable tow placed around his waist and then finally the hoodwink. These days it is just the hoodwink.

After having proved himself to be a Master Mason, the candidate is given the passwords to enable him to proceed.

The import of these curious words, communicated to us before we enter a Royal Arch Chapter for the first time, is something we do not tend to give a lot of thought to. In some Chapters we only hear these words when we are candidates and the Principal Sojourner gives them to us before we enter to be exalted but, in others, the Scribe Nehemiah stands at the door and demands them from every Companion as he enters before the Chapter is open.

So where do these words come from and what do they mean?

To partially answer the second question first, they do not mean what we are told they mean. They are taken from the Book of the Prophet Hosea. Hosea lived in northern Israel in the 8th century BC. At God's command, he married a prostitute called Gomer who was unfaithful to him. Hosea brought her back and forgave her and this enabled him to draw a parallel with Israel's infidelity to the True God by worshipping other, polytheistic gods. Hosea said that God would forgive Israel if she repented.

Some time later, in around 587 BC, Nebuchadnezzar, King of Babylon, destroyed the Temple of King Solomon and took the Israelites into captivity. Our Royal Arch story begins when three Sojourners arrive, 70 years later, having been freed to join Zerubbabel, Haggai and Joshua back in their native land, and ask to participate in the rebuilding of the Temple. The fact that they and the august Sanhedrin are in Jerusalem at all is due to the mercy of God, expressed through Cyrus, King of Persia, who had conquered Babylon and – partly for political reasons – had let the Israelites return to their own country.

The literal meaning of 'A, R' is 'Brothers and sisters' and that is what it says in the second chapter of the Book of Hosea. It is only in the Douai Rheims (Roman Catholic) version of the Bible that the words 'My people have found mercy' appear. It is at this point that the Volume of the Sacred Law should be opened in a Royal Arch Chapter.

So the Jews had made things right with God and were allowed by His mercy to return to their native land in the period between 538 and 520 BC. But things were never the same again. Some did not return and this was the beginning of the Jewish diaspora. Jehoiachim, for instance, the King of Judah when the exile in Babylon began, who is mentioned in the colloquy between the First Principal and the Principal Sojourner, spent 37 years in a Babylonian prison and then elected to remain in Babylon for the rest of his life. Moreover the era of prophecy was largely over and the scribes took over as interpreters and expounders of the sacred law which became known as the Torah – the basis of Judaism to this day.

It is worth noting that the words given above were only adopted after 1835 when the Royal Arch was opened up to all Master Masons and not just to Installed Masters as had previously been the case, when the word required would be the word of an Installed Master. A substitute word or words had to be found and the First Grand Principal, The Duke of Sussex, consulted the Chief Rabbi who was a friend of his and these words were devised.[49]

The Ceremony of Exaltation begins

The candidate is then announced by the Janitor and received, blindfolded, into the Chapter by the Sojourners in the west. A prayer is said and then the candidate's bona fides are tested before he is led round the Chapter in the form of an arch. I remember once seeing this done where the Assistant Sojourner walked in front and pulled out each alternate banner so the candidate's progress was zigzagged. There is also a Chapter in Cambridge where the candidate is made to touch the pedestal and step on the implements as he passes. Neville Barker Cryer explains this as follows:

> It is therefore important that he should also learn that he is not being led round a SQUARE space as was the case previously. At the very least he needs to be led up one pillar and by the curve of an arch before he returns along another pillar. What may be a surprise to you is the fact that in places as far apart as Cambridge and Preston, Lancashire, it is still the practice for the Royal Arch candidate to be led from the west a short way up the north, passing then to the south over the floorcloth and through the staves, up to the east where the curve of the arch is made, down the north and again through the staves to the south before turning right to the west. Why do they still retain this 18th century practice? The answer is that this was the sort of route that an Antient Mason would have taken in his search for a keystone that was lost. Since the Royal Arch was closely allied to Mark Masonry as its preparation these Chapters preserve this form of their perambulation to remind a candidate of what he would already have experienced as a Mark Master Mason. They then add the further feature of a Catenarian arch in the East to indicate 'the further progress he is to make in the science'. The form and use of the perambulation should be seen as very important indeed.

So right from the beginning we see that we have now graduated from square perambulations to tracing the form of an arch, either in the normal way or by making a sort of figure-of-eight as above.

---

49 Fraternity Chapter No.4072 – *Exaltation with Explanation* by Rev Neville Barker Cryer (2002)

Having arrived back in the west, the candidate is instructed to advance towards the shrine on which the sacred name is deposited by seven steps. He halts and bows at the third, fifth and seventh and this is a vestige of the ceremony of Passing of the Veils, described in Chapter 11. There are three steps to the blue veil, two to the purple veil and a final two to the crimson veil. The colours are those of the veils of the Tabernacle and later the Temple which were passed to reveal the true name of God. Red or crimson and dark blue are of course the colours of the Royal Arch, as we see from our regalia, the robes of our Principals etc., and when those two are combined we get purple. Seven steps also symbolise Jacob's seven-rung ladder, as portrayed on Craft Tracing Boards and the Seven Corporal Works of Mercy described in the Book of Isaiah chapter 15 vv1–12:

- To feed the hungry.
- To give drink to the thirsty.
- To shelter the homeless.
- To clothe the naked.
- To visit and ransom the captive (prisoners).
- To visit the sick.
- To bury the dead.

The first six of these are taken from St.Matthew's Gospel Chapter 25 vv31-46 and the final one is from the apocryphal Book of Tobit.

When the candidate gets to the shrine (i.e. the arch) he is informed that he has arrived at the crown of a vaulted chamber and that he must knock out two of the arch stones and figuratively descend into it.

We may also note the white robes of the Scribes and the white cloth covering the altar. These are vestiges of the white veil, the last to be passed in the Veils ceremony, behind which the genuine secrets were to be found.

The next thing that happens is that the candidate kneels to hear a portion of scripture taken from the Book of Proverbs. He is told it is *a portion of the writings of our Grand Master, King Solomon.* This is because King Solomon was originally credited as being the author of Proverbs which were called in the original Hebrew *Míshlê Shlomoh* or Proverbs of Solomon, although there may have been other contributing authors. The authorship of at least part of the book by Solomon is certainly confirmed by the first verse of the first chapter:

The proverbs of Solomon son of David, king of Israel.

The passage describes the virtues of wisdom and understanding, leading to righteousness, judgement, equity and every good path.

This, when you think about it, is what we are trying to acquire by our Exaltation. We seek the genuine secrets of Masonry and, in obtaining them, to get a better understanding of our relationship with God.

Albert Pike says: *It is WISDOM that, in the Kabalistic Books of the Proverbs & Ecclesiastes, is the Creative Agent of God. Elsewhere in the Hebrew writings it is Debar Iahavah, the Word of God. It is by His uttered Word that God reveals Himself to us; not only in the visible & invisible but intellectual creation, but also in our convictions, consciousness, & instincts. Hence it is that certain beliefs are universal.*[50]

The candidate is then instructed to find something in the vault which turns out to be a scroll of vellum or parchment. He cannot read the scroll because he lacks light (he is of course still hoodwinked). The candidate is instructed to rise, wrench forth the keystone and then kneel again to hear a reading from the Book of Haggai.

This reading is a lot different from the first one. The prophet is exhorting Zerubbabel and Joshua the High Priest to have strength and to build an even greater Temple than the one King Solomon built. He assures them that God is still with them, despite the fact that His physical presence over the Ark of the Covenant has gone.

So the keystone and two contiguous arch stones are taken out and the candidate is ready to be obligated. Of course you don't need to be a chartered engineer to realise that if you had knocked out the two contiguous arch stones and left the keystone in situ the whole thing would collapse and that is why the arch stones in our chapters are usually arranged on semi-circular hoops, but then this is a fictional account! Cryer claims that this is based on a combination of two legends: one relating to the Arches of Enoch (see Introduction and elsewhere) and the other concerned with a vaulted crypt where Hiram Abif was buried.

After that, the candidate prepares to take his obligation, supporting the VSL in his left hand and with his right hand upon it. Supporting the VSL in this way harks back to a time when there were no desks or pedestals on which to place the sacred volume and this gave rise to the due guard, still used in Scotland, and made before giving the sign of the degree which shows the position the hands were in whilst the obligation was being taken.

He promises never to reveal the secrets of the Degree, as is normal, but also that he will not pronounce the sacred name of God (when he gets it) except in strictly defined circumstances. It is interesting to note that we ourselves refer to God throughout the ceremony as the TALGMH and not by His Name, which only the Principals, or two of the Principals and the newly exalted candidate as we shall see later, can pronounce between the three of them.

The obligation completed, the candidate is raised by the Principal Sojourner and restored to light. The sight that greets him when this

---

50 *Morals and Dogma* by Albert Pike

happens is truly magnificent to behold. He should not have seen a Royal Arch Chapter laid out before and the sight of the artefacts, illuminated only by the Six Lights is a very memorable one. For that reason his proposer and seconder should ensure that he does not wander into the Temple before the ceremony.

But, let's linger at this point and note a couple of things. First of all the manner in which the Principal Sojourner raises the candidate is a curious one. It comprises five movements (remember the number five was key in early Royal Arch ceremonies and we still have five signs etc.) and the positions in which the Sojourner grips the candidate is similar, if not in every respect identical to the different grips used in the Ceremony of Passing of the Veils (see Chapter 11). What is happening is that the candidate is being raised not merely from a kneeling stool but out of a vault!

The Companions are tilting the banner poles on which the tribal banners are hung and the Principals form a triangle with their sceptres. Cryer claims that this tilting represents the arches leading to the altar and that the right-angled triangular formation of the sceptres was the central secret of the mediaeval master architects.[51] The old legend talks of nine arches but, as we have already seen and will see again in the dramatic portion of the ceremony, we are only dealing with seven. So here, when the candidate is restored to light, he sees twelve tribal banners being tilted (i.e. six pairs) plus the triangle being formed by the Principals' sceptres, making seven arches in all.

In some Chapters the two Scribes will stand at the eastern end of the banners and after the drama has been played out will uncover the altar, relieving it of its white veil (usually edged with a gold trim). The Scribes wear white robes and these and the altar cover are vestiges of the fourth or white veil (again see Chapter 11).

Having given the candidate a moment to assimilate what he is now seeing the First Principal congratulates him on being admitted to the light of Royal Arch Masonry, and invites him to read the words on the scroll he brought out of the vault. At one time the words on the scroll came from the first chapter of St. John's Gospel: *In the beginning was the Word and the Word was with God and the Word was God. However, now that the Royal Arch is open to men of all faiths we use the first chapter of the Book of Genesis verses 1-3: In the beginning God created heaven and earth and the earth was without form and void; and darkness was upon the face of the deep. And the Spirit of God moved on the face of the waters and God said 'Let there be light' and there was light. This is of course why one side of our arch stones bear the Latin inscription Fiat Lux. The quotation in full is Fiat*

---

51   Fraternity Chapter No.4072 – *Exaltation with Explanation* by Rev Neville Barker Cryer (2002)

lux et lux fuit, meaning 'let there be light and there was light'.

In the Complete Working the Second and Third Principals add to what has already been said by the First Principal by first of all encapsulating the teachings of the Craft and saying that the ceremony of Raising implies that there is more to learn and then describing how the Royal Arch develops this theme.

At this point the candidate will retire with the Principal and First Assistant Sojourners to begin the dramatic portion of the ceremony. In former times the candidate would have undergone the ceremony of Passing of the Veils (see Chapter 11) and would then have come in and been obligated before this point.

The Drama

The Chapter is restored to light and the Sojourners and candidate return, wearing Master Masons' aprons and state what they have come for.

The Grand Sanhedrin (a misnomer because the Jewish Sanhedrin did not exist before 79 BC which is long after our period) is a little hesitant at first until, in typical Jewish fashion at that time, the Sojourners prove their antecedents and that they were not among those who fled, in Nebuchadnezzar's time from the approaching Babylonian army or of the Tribe left behind for the purpose of tilling the land (who later became the Samaritans) but are of good lineage dating back to the patriarch Abraham. More than satisfied with this the Sanhedrin informs the Sojourners that the work of rebuilding has already begun but they may go and excavate in the ruins of the old Temple and report back. The Sojourners thank the Sanhedrin for their trust and the Scribes give them the pick, crow and shovel as the requisite working implements. They will retire and the Principal Sojourner will take two lengths of rope, the uses of which he will describe later.

A little while later there will be an alarm (not with the Master Mason's knocks as before, but with four distinct knocks – recalling that the Antients' Grand Lodge considered the Royal Arch as nothing other than the Fourth Degree in Freemasonry) and the Janitor will announce that the Three Sojourners who were sent to clear the ground have made a discovery of importance and, in line with what they were told before they retired, must communicate it to the Grand Sanhedrin only.

They are re-admitted and asked to explain their findings. The Principal Sojourner recounts that they found an arch and pulled out two of the arch stones. We should note that this is an Arch Degree but the legend is about a vault. He goes on to describe what was found at his first and then second descent, at which they discovered the pedestal of white marble with its plate of gold. This plate of gold is very significant because there was a plate of gold on top of the Ark of the Covenant. Mention of that has been dropped from our ritual now (and it is no longer appearing on our Grand Chapter certificates, although it once did), but the implication is that the Ark is still there.[52]

According to Hoyos, there are three legends similar to ours which we have already looked at in Chapter 3, but none of them makes reference to plate of gold, which is obviously key to the whole ceremony.

The Grand Sanhedrin is suitably impressed and instructs the Scribes to go and check it out.

The Principal Sojourner accompanies Scribes Ezra and Nehemiah to a corner of the room outside the hearing of the candidate (Metropolitan ritual recommends that they actually leave the room for this purpose) to share the fruits of their discovery. The Scribes report to the Principals that the genuine secret has indeed been found.

Investment

The candidate is then invested, rewarded, decorated and entrusted.

He is invested with what is called a badge, rather than an apron, because at one time it was a badge attached to a Craft apron to show that he was Royal Arch. This was discontinued after 1835 when Royal Arch regalia was introduced.

He is rewarded with the jewel of a Royal Arch Mason and admitted with approbation within the Grand Sanhedrim.

He is decorated with the ribbon or sash which, as we have already seen, is composed of the colours of the veils of the Temple and is worn over the left shoulder, which also explains why the P——l sign is given with the left hand.

Finally he is entrusted with a Staff of Office which he will 'always be permitted to bear unless seventy-two of your elders are present'. This appears a curious stipulation until you look into it. Seventy-two is a number of great significance, as is every number in the Bible.

The Book of Numbers gives an account of Moses' gathering seventy elders of Israel, who received a share of Moses' spirit and would assist him in leading the people. Some say that two of them, Eldad and Medad, were outside the camp when the seventy received the spirit but got a portion nevertheless. Others say that it was 70 plus Aaron and Moses making seventy-two, who spoke on God's behalf to the people.

---

52 *The Mystery of the Royal Arch Word* by Arturo de Hoyos – Pietre-Stones Review of Freemasonry

It has also been noted that there were 72 ornaments on the Menorah in the Tabernacle – a symbol of Light – and the oil in it, symbolic of the Holy Spirit. Additionally, there were said to be 72 separate pieces of the veil in the Temple which separated the Holy place from the Most Holy Place. The garment of the High Priest has brass bells and pomegranates woven into its hem. Interestingly, they have decided that 72 of each, alternating around the hem, will be used.

There are in the Book of Exodus three verses in the fourteenth chapter, describing the pillars of fire and of cloud forming a defence unto the children of Israel against the Egyptians. Each of these three verses consists in the Hebrew of seventy-two letters, and by writing them in a certain manner one above another, seventy-two columns of three letters each are obtained; each column is then treated as a Name of Three Letters, and the explanation of these is sought for in certain verses of the Psalms which contain these Names; and these latter would be the verses of the Psalms alluded to in the text, which the seventy-two poor persons were told to recite.

It doesn't finish with the Old Testament either. In Luke 10:1–12, 72 apostles, additional to the original 12 are sent out in pairs to preach the Gospel.

From the Kabbalah we discover a method of investigating the natures of the Name of God in the four letters found on the top of our altar, which is considered to contain all the Forces of Nature.

In Metropolitan ritual the order of investment is jewel, ribbon, badge and finally the staff, but the end result is the same.

The words said at the end of this address are of great significance: *We hereby constitute you Princes and Rulers amongst us.* So these three guys who came down from Babylon prepared to do a labouring job have now been admitted to the Grand Sanhedrim of the Jewish people, not merely as Companions but as Princes and Rulers, in recognition of the discovery they have made.

Just what, then, are the genuine secrets of Freemasonry? What is it that we find by joining a Royal Arch Chapter that we did not learn in the Craft? Well, the secrets are more or less the same whether in Craft, Mark or anywhere else. First let's ask ourselves what does a degree consist of?

There is usually some sort of proving to show that the candidate is what he says he is. Then there is a prayer, an advance usually to the east but in the case of the Royal Arch to the arch stones in the west. This is followed by an obligation, the conferment of the secrets peculiar to the degree – sign, token and word – a further proving, some working tools and usually some sort of lecture. That is the bare bones of what a degree is, albeit with variations. In the Royal Arch there is, in between the obligation and the conferment of secrets, a drama. But it boils down to the same thing in the end. There are five signs in the Royal Arch, two tokens – that by which the candidate is raised by the Principal Sojourner and that between the candidate and the Principals and later by the Principals alone – and of course the word is the ultimate quest which we have now completed. The working tools are the pick, crow and shovel which are described in the Symbolical Lecture.

Royal Arch Regalia

This seems a good place to look at the regalia worn by Royal Arch Masons. It consists throughout one's Royal Arch career of an apron, sash and jewel, although the colours will change with advancement. The skin of the apron, as with all Masonic aprons, is white denoting purity and innocence and was at one time made from lambskin. As a Companion the belt and the hangings are also white, with the seven gold tassels which are said to derive from the apron strings once used to tie Masonic aprons but also symbolise a number of other things in Craft Masonry.[53] To further develop that, we might note that we take seven steps towards the Sacred Name in the Royal Arch.

Excellent Companion Roger T. Quayle, Deputy Grand Superintendent, Cheshire.

The sash with its ornamentation of red and blue/purple diamonds, denoting the colours of the veils of the Temple (and also the veils once used in the ceremony), is worn over the left shoulder. Some say this is because no sword is worn so it is over the left shoulder in contrast to a Knight Templar and other sashes, worn over the right. I take issue with this because we are taught in the Symbolical Lecture that a sword WAS worn: *With a sword in their left hand and a trowel in their right, they stood ever ready to defend the city and Holy Temple from the unprovoked attacks of their aggressors.* So, if you have got to hold the sword in your left hand you would carry it in a sheath hung from a sash on your right hip, which accounts for the sash being over the left shoulder.

On becoming a Principal and thereby an Excellent Companion, the colour changes from white to red: the ribbon on the jewel, the hangings on the apron, the apron belt and the triangular

---

53 *A Guide to Masonic Symbolism* by the present author

piece behind the Triple Tau on the sash. As I know from running a regalia shop, it is surprising how many Companions do not realise that it is not only the colour of the jewel that changes when they are elevated to a Principal of their Chapter.

Some years after coming out of the Z Chair of your Chapter (not usually less than five, depending on where you are in the world) you may be awarded Provincial, Metropolitan or District Grand rank. Then the items cited above change from red to dark blue, except for the breast jewel which becomes tricolour (the colours of the veils again). You also get a tricolour collarette with a jewel of rank appended to it and an apron badge to reflect the rank to which you are appointed.

Sometimes, usually after a couple of promotions, comes the ultimate accolade of Grand rank. Colours do not change but the apron becomes bigger, with the badge of rank sewn in and the collarette becomes a collar.

The regalia of a Grand Chapter Officer.

I should of course mention that the Royal Arch jewel (whatever the colour of the ribbon) should not only be worn in Chapter but also in one's Craft lodge. A Brother failing to do so is improperly dressed. Many lodge summonses these days invite a Brother interested in the Royal Arch to approach any other Brother who is wearing a Royal Arch jewel for further information. This is no longer really satisfactory because the Brother/Companion thus approached may have only been exalted last week. It is far better to have some sort of Royal Arch liaison officer within the Lodge and for his details to appear on the summons.

The Closing of the Chapter

Having conducted the routine business of correspondence, approval of accounts, propositions for concluded and the Chapter is ready to be closed.

In most rituals the closing consists of the Three Principals placing their hands on the VSL and uttering the time-honoured words 'We all do meet and agree' etc. Then the First Principal instructs the Principal Sojourner to close the Chapter, which he does after the Principals have given their sceptres to the DC who lays them on the floor in the shape of a triangle with the apex pointing towards the east. The Principals then say: Z: Glory to God in the Highest, H: On earth peace, J: Goodwill towards men. The practice of raising and lowering the hands at this point is not well understood but it has been suggested as symbolic of sharing the Sacred Name. The IPZ will confirm that the Chapter is closed, much as the IPM would do in a Craft lodge.

But there are still some interesting variations to closing ceremonies. In Amphibious Chapter No.258 in the Province of Yorkshire (West Riding) not only the Principals form a group of three during the closing, the Sojourners at the western end do it as well and then the VSL is passed round the Chapter to be saluted by all present. In St.Lawrence Chapter No.2330, also in Yorkshire (West Riding) and also in St.Paul's Chapter No.2277 in Nicosia, Cyprus, ALL the Companions present form into groups of three and salute the book while sharing the closing words.

But Royal Forest Chapter No.401 (1999 ritual) go even further. They have a colloquy between the First Principal and other officers rather like the closing of a Craft lodge, in which Z first asks the Principal Sojourner to direct the Scribe Nehemiah to ascertain that the Chapter is properly tyled, then asks the Scribe Nehemiah what the next care is. The Companions are instructed to come to order as Royal Arch Masons by showing – but not holding – the R or H sign. Z then asks the Third Principal whence he comes and the answer is:

From exploring among the ruins of the First Temple, Most Excellent.

Z then asks the Second Principal if he has been successful in the object of his search, to which H replies:

We have, Most Excellent. We have recovered the long lost genuine secrets of a Master Mason and are anxious to impart them to your Excellency.

Then H and J communicate the word as in the Exaltation ceremony, the words 'We three etc' are spoken and the DC instructs the Sojourners to also share the word, after which all the Companions salute the VSL. The closing prayer then used is most unusual:

Supreme and Incomprehensible I AM, may the sincerity of our feeble exertions meet with Thy divine approbation, may our efforts to disseminate knowledge of Thyself, and of Thine attributes be crowned with success, and may our Order be blessed with peace and firm continuance, through Thine almighty protection.

A very original prayer indeed!

After everything else has been done, the Principal Sojourner then has the last word, paraphrasing the Book of Ecclesiastes:

Companions, this is the conclusion of the whole business, fear God and keep His commandments, for this is the whole duty of man.

In some rituals a Valedictory Address is given after the Chapter is closed but before the Companions have separated as follows:

You are now about to quit this sacred retreat of friendship and virtue and mix again with the world. Amidst its concerns and employments forget not the duties you have heard forcibly and so frequently inculcated in our meetings. Be ye therefore diligent, prudent, temperate and discreet; remember also that around our pedestal you have solemnly and repeatedly engaged yourselves to befriend and relieve with unhesitating cordiality, so far as shall be in your power, every brother who shall need your assistance. That you have promised to remind him in the most tender manner of his failings and aid his reformation. To vindicate his character when wrongly traduced and to suggest on his behalf the most candid, favourable and palliating circumstances in extenuation of his conduct even when justly reprehended; that the world may observe and feel how truly Masons love one another.

These generous principles ought to extend beyond the limited arena of our society, for every human being has a claim to our good offices, so that we enjoin you to do good unto all, but more especially unto the household of the faithful. By diligence in the duties of your respective callings, by liberal benevolence and diffusive charity, by constancy and fidelity in your friendship, by uniformly just, amiable and virtuous deportment, we charge you to manifest the beneficial effects of our ancient and honourable institution. And let it not be supposed, Brethren, that you will labour in vain or spend your strength for nought; for your work will be with the Lord and your recompense with God. Finally, brethren, be ye of one heart and one mind; love one another and live in peace. And may the God of love and peace delight to dwell with you and to bless you.

CHAPTER 9

The Royal Arch Lectures Explained

Introduction

Early in the 19th century the lectures of the Royal Arch were in five sections. I am reproducing them here from the *Manual of Freemasonry* (which was actually an exposure) by Richard Carlile (1790-1843) because we get clear indications from them as to whence our present RA ceremony came. Not only that, but when this manual first appeared around 1825, there were no printed rituals, as we now know them, so whilst it is true to say that anyone could buy the book for two shillings and sixpence (12½p), a lot of the buyers would probably have been Masons because printed rituals are very useful as we all know.

Carlile's Royal Arch Lectures

The second section of these Lectures concerned the Passing of the Veils and is discussed in Chapter 11. There is much of interest, however, in the remaining four sections.

The Lectures are in catechetical form and the first section is as follows:

Q. *Are you a Royal Arch Mason?*

A. *I am.*

Q. *How shall I know you to be such?*

A. *By the Royal Arch sign.*

Q. *Can you give me that sign?*

A. *I can (gives it)*

Q. *Where did you learn that sign?*

A. *In a Royal Arch Chapter.*

Q. *Who were present?*

A. *The Three Principals, Zerubbabel the Prince of the people, Haggai the Prophet and Jeshua the High Priest, with the rest of the Companions, men chosen for virtue and moral rectitude; the better to enable them to superintend the carrying on of the works of the Second Temple.*

Q. *How did you gain admittance?*

A. *By having been initiated into the first degree of Masonry as an Entered Apprentice, passed to the Degree of a Fellow-Craft, raised to the sublime Degree of a Master Mason, by being in possession of a Past Master's word and signs.*

Q. *Do you recollect the Past Master's word?*

A. *I do*

Q. *Will you give it to me?*

A. –

Q. *What does that word denote?*

A. –

Q. *When admitted, how were you placed?*

A. *On both knees, to receive the benefit of a prayer.*

Q. *How were you then disposed of?*

A. *I was led to the altar, where the Prophet Haggai received me, and gave me an exhortation.*

Q. *Can you give me the substance of it?*

A. *I can : That as I was about to undertake a solemn and glorious work in entering into an obligation before the Grand Sanhedrim, it was essential that sincerity and truth should accompany all the future undertakings of my life.*

Q. *Did you enter into that obligation?*

A. *I did after the High Priest had read a portion of Scripture [Proverbs 2, as now]*

Q. *Can you repeat the obligation?*

A. *I can:*

'I, A.B., of my own free will and accord, in the presence of the Grand Architect of the Universe, and this Chapter of Royal Arch Masons, do hereby and hereon most solemnly and sincerely promise and swear, in addition to my former obligations, that I will not reveal the secrets of this degree to anyone of an inferior degree, or to any one except he be a true and lawful Companion Royal Arch Mason, or within the body of a just and legally constituted chapter, under the penalty of having the crown of my skull struck off, in addition to all my former penalties. So help me God, and keep me firm in this my obligation of a Royal Arch Companion' [The Bible was then kissed five times.]

Q. *What was then required of you?*

A. *In whom did I put my trust?*

Q. *Your answer?*

A. *In Jehovah.*

Q. *Why were you obligated?*

A. *To teach me to avoid the offences committed by our ancestors, who deviating from true Masonic principles and laws, brought on themselves and their posterity that heavy burthen (sic), and on their city and temple that ruin and desolation, whereby the holy word was so long lost, and afterwards so miraculously discovered.*

Q. *What was next said to you?*

A. *I was ordered to arise in the name of that Omnipotent Being, and the Principal, Zerubbabel, delivered the following exordium:*

'Companions, the Masonic system exhibits a stupendous and beautiful fabric, founded on universal wisdom, unfolding its gates to receive, without prejudice or discrimination, the worthy professors of every description of genuine religion and knowledge; concentrating as it were into one body their just tenets, unencumbered

with the disputable peculiarities of any sect or persuasion. This system originated in the earliest of ages, and among the wisest of men. But it is to be lamented, that to the desponding suggestions of some of the weaker minds among our own fraternity, the prejudices of the world against our invaluable institution are in a great measure imputable. Unable to comprehend the beautiful allegories of ancient wisdom, they ignorantly assert that the rites of Masonry are futile; its doctrines inefficient. To this assertion, indeed, they give, by their own misconduct, a semblance of truth, as we fail to discern that they are made wiser or better men by their admission to our mysteries.

' Companions, I need not tell you, that nature alone can provide us with the ground of wisdom; but Masonry will teach and enable us to cultivate the soil, and to foster and strengthen the plant in its growth. Therefore, to dispel the clouds of ignorance, so inauspicious to the noble purposes of our order and to hold forth a moral whereby we may see the power and greatness of the all-wise Disposer of events, the Royal Arch Degree gives us an ample field for discussion, by which we are shown, in the sad experience of the once-favourite people of God, a lesson, how to conduct ourselves in every situation of our existence; and that when fortune, affluence, sickness or adversity attend us, we ought never to lose sight of the source from whence it came, always remembering that the power which gave is also a power to take away. Having in itself this grand moral, which ought to be cultivated by every man among us – 'to do unto others as we would wish to be done by' and it is the ultimatum of all terrestrial happiness, imitating in itself every virtue that man can possess. May we, as Companions, so study virtue as to hand it down to posterity a name unspotted by vice and worthy of imitation.'

Q. How were you then disposed of?

A. I was desired to retire, to be further prepared.

End of First Section

Commentary

There are no real surprises here. Firstly the candidate is received by the Prophet Haggai who appears to be the main man. Secondly it is necessary for the candidate to give the word of an Installed Master because he would have had to have passed the chair to join the Royal Arch in those days and indeed would have required that word to become a Principal until 2004. It would appear that the second Scripture reading (from the Book of Haggai) has replaced the exhortation given by Haggai in the ceremony. The exordium, which has long since gone, seems to be summing up the first scripture reading from the Book of Proverbs.

Second Section – see Chapter 11 Passing of the Veils

Q. *Were you instructed as to what they meant?*

A. *We were. Zerubbabel informed us that the mysterious characters within the double triangle were the long-lost word of a Master Mason and too incomprehensible for individual expression; but that in reward for our industry and zeal, we should be put in possession of a full explanation of this, the Grand Omnific Word of a Royal Arch Mason. We were further told that as the drawing of the third keystone obtained us the grand omnific word, it had been so obtained by the prayer, which was an emblem of drawing the first and the obligation which was an emblem of drawing the second keystone, as similitudes of material things.*

Q. *Were you then invested?*

A. *I was invested with the sash and apron of a Royal Arch Mason: and also invested with the various branches of their laws and mysteries.*

End of Third Section

Commentary

Here we can clearly see the origins of our present ceremony. Bear in mind that our story is part fiction and part fact. The return to Jerusalem under Zerubbabel and Joshua is biblically correct but the three Sojourners and their discovery is not and is part of the story composed to facilitate a finding of secrets lost at the death of Hiram Abif.

Note the use of the term Junior Sojourner. In those days there was a Principal, a Senior and a Junior Sojourner, rather than a Principal and first and second Assistant Sojourners as now.

A couple of other things are worth noting. Firstly we are told that Cyrus the Great converted to the worship of the One True God, which is something not mentioned in our ceremony. Secondly the Sojourners here delve through three arches to find the pedestal with the plate of gold. Then there is the matter of the 'Grand Omnific Word' – a rather dated phrase. Omnific means capable of making or doing anything and John Milton uses it in Paradise Lost:

Silence, ye troubl'd waves, and thou Deep, peace, Said then th' Omnific Word

It has recently resurfaced in the creative names of certain business enterprises: Omnific Publishing, Omnific Interior Design, etc., but the word has generally fallen into disuse. The grand word referred to is obviously the three-syllable compound word referred to elsewhere.

We should also note that the candidate is invested with a sash and an apron. There is no mention of a jewel or a staff of office.

Fourth Section

Q. *What are you?*

A. *A citizen of the world, a brother to every worthy Mason and a companion to those of our Royal Arch Degree.*

Q. *Pray, Sojourner, who are you?*

A. *Of your own kindred and people, sprung from the noble and illustrious race of ancestors whose honours we hope to merit, by a steady pursuit of wisdom, truth and justice.*

Q. *From whence came you?*

A. *From the Grand Royal Arch Chapter of Jerusalem.*

Q. *Who were present?*

A. *Zerubbabel the Prince of the people, Haggai the prophet and Jeshua the High Priest.*

Q. *What do the Principals of a Royal Arch Chapter represent?*

A. *Zerubbabel, Haggai and Jeshua represent the three keystones, by which we learn in drawing them forth, the discovery is complete; and by the passing of the Sojourners through each of these offices, the mystical knowledge of our Royal Arch Chapter is obtained.*

Q. *What do the two scribes represent?*

A. *The two scribes, Ezra and Nehemiah, representing the two columns or pillars that supported the entrance of the arch; and thereby also is signified their duty of registering and entering on our records every act, law or transaction for the general good of the chapter.*

Q. *What do the three Sojourners represent?*

A. *The three Sojourners represent the three stones whereon the three Grand Masters knelt to offer up their prayers for the success of their work. And hereby we have a lesson that in everything we undertake we ought to offer up our prayers to the Almighty for success.*

Q. *Why do we, as Royal Arch Masons, sit in this form?*

A. *To represent the Holy Royal Arch; and hereby we have a lesson to pursue unity and concord; for as one stone drawn from an arch endangers the whole, so may the improper conduct of one member endanger the whole chapter.*

Q. *Why was the ceremony of drawing the three keystones observed?*

A. *To teach us not to rely on our own reasoning and abilities for our conduct through life; but to draw forth our rules or government from the law and the prophets, and also to commemorate the discovery of the Royal Arch.*

Q. *What was this part of their discovery?*

A. *The pedestal of perfect white marble, worked in the form of a double cube. On the top a plate of gold containing the figure of a triple triangle. Within the figure are the mysterious characters, which the Grand and Royal Chapter informed us were the grand omnific word itself.*

Q. *Were you entrusted with the grand word?*

A. *I was. They gave e the grand movement, taught me the sign and entrusted e with the sacred word, which is too incomprehensible for an individual to express.*

Q. *Was that word ever lost?*

A. *It was.*

Q. *In what manner?*

A. *By the untimely death of our Grand Master, Hiram Abif, who was slain by a conspiracy of the craft, in order to extort it from him; therefore as the word was incomprehensible without the three Grand Masters being present, another word was substituted in its room, until the Grand Architect of the universe caused it to be discovered.*

Q. *How was that discovery made?*

A. *By the three Sojourners preparing for the foundation of the second temple, who made the report thereof to the Royal Arch Chapter. As the labourers were clearing away the rubbish, they perceived the crown of an arch. At the time of the destruction of the temple, the roof and walls fell in and remained full seventy years a heap of rubbish. The arch, being unknown to any but the three Grand Masters, was their secret and royal council room. It was made and remained proof against the destroying flames and fury of the enemy, until the discovery was made and its contents known.*

Q. *At what time did that discovery happen?*

A. *The discovery was made in the first year of Cyrus, King of Persia and Babylon, on the return of the Jews from the Babylonish captivity. The three Sojourners discovered the pedestal perfect and entire, having withstood the fury of the flames and rage of war, being defended by HIM who having declared that he would place his word there, never to pass away. Hence we learn the vanity of all human pursuits against the arm of Omnipotence.*

End of Fourth Section

Commentary

On the face of it, there is nothing much in this section that we do not already know about from our modern RA ceremony. However, there are one or two points we should note. The idea of the three Sojourners representing three stones on which the Three Grand Masters knelt to offer prayer for the success of their endeavours is no longer known to us, but is an interesting bit of symbolism.

The clearing of the ground during the first year of the reign of Cyrus (although we know this part to be fictitious) would have been unlikely anyway because, as we have seen, work on rebuilding the Temple did not commence immediately after the first wave of return.

Fifth Section

Q. *Can you describe the grand pedestal?*

A. *It was on a chequered pavement, to represent the uncertainty of life and the* instability of things terrestrial. It was of perfect white marble, cut into the form of an altar of incense, being the true double cube and thereby both in figure and colour the most perfect emblem of innocence and purity. On the base of the pedestal is the letter 'G', which signifies [the word of an Installed Master] a common name for all Masons who are masters of their business. Hereby we have a lesson of humility and brotherly love: for there is no doubt it was most highly finished, as the work of the great Hiram Abif himself; he would not assume the honour, but affix the common name, that every companion might be a sharer. On the front were inscribed the names of the three most excellent grand masters. On the top was a plate of gold in which was engraved a triple triangle and within the figure the grand omnific word.

Q. Can you explain the jewel?

A. On the bottom of the scroll is inscribed the motto Nil nisi clavis deest – nothing but the key is wanting; which may be taken in its literal sense. Then the circle is an emblem of eternity with the motto: Talia si jungere possis, sit tibi scire satis – if thou canst comprehend these things, thou knowest enough. The two intersecting triangles denote the elements of fire and water, with a motto declaring that the wearer is desirous of doing his duty and filling up with justice that link in the chain of creation wherein his Creator had thought fit to place him. Within is another triangle, with the sun in its centre, its rays issuing forth at every point, an emblem of the Deity represented by a circle, whose centre is everywhere and circumference nowhere, denoting His omnipresence and perfection. It is also an emblem of geometry. And here we find the most perfect emblem of the science of agriculture: not a partial one, like the Basilidean, calculated for one particular climate or country: but universal pointed out by a pair of compasses issuing from the centre of the sun, and suspending a globe denoting the earth, and thereby representing the influence of that glorious luminary over both the animal and vegetable creation: admonishing us to be careful to perform every operation in its proper season, that we lose not the fruits of our labour. Under these is the compound character [T surmounting H] or the Royal Arch Masons' badge.

Q. What explanation can you give of this deeply mystical character?

A. It signifies in its figurative appearance as T. H., Templum Hierosolyma, the Temple of Jerusalem, and is always used as the Royal Arch Mason's badge, by which the wearer acknowledges himself a servant of the true God, who had thereby established His worship, and to Whose service that glorious temple was erected. It also signifies Clavis ad Thesaurum – a key to a treasure and Theca ubi res pretiosa deponitur – a place where a precious thing is concealed; or Res ipsa pretiosa, the precious thing itself. Hence we have the greatest reason to believe that what was there concealed was the sacred name itself. But these are all symbolic definitions of the symbol, which is to be simply solved into an emblem of science in the human mind, and is the most ancient symbol of that kind, the prototype of the cross and the first object in every religion or human system of worship. *This is the grand secret of Masonry, which passes by symbols from superstition to science: as ignorance dealing with ancient mysteries and symbols passes from science to superstition.*

Q. Explain the five grand original signs.

A. *The first parents of mankind, formed by the Grand Architect of the Universe, in the utmost perfection both of body and mind, seated in a paradise of pleasure, bounteously supplied with means for the gratification of every appetite and at full liberty for enjoyment to the end of time itself, with only one prohibition by way of contract whereon should depend their immortality, soon became disobedient and thereby obnoxious to sin, misery and death. To preserve us from which, and as a memento to guard us from the like error, we adopted the venal sign.*

Scarcely had our first parents transgressed, conscious of their crime and filled with shame and horror, they endeavoured to hide themselves from the presence of that Being in whom before had been their chief delight; but hearing the summons of His awful voice and unable to bear the splendour of His appearance, in a humble bending posture they approached with awe and palpitation of the heart, their right hand at their forehead for support and their left at the heart as a shield against the radiant glory; and hence arose the reverential sign or sign of salute.

It was now they heard pronounced the dreadful sentence that the ground, for their sakes accursed should no longer pour forth in such abundance; but themselves be driven from that happy region to some less friendly climate there to cultivate the hungry soil and to earn their daily food by sweat and labour. Now banished from the presence of God, and impelled by the wants and calls of nature to constant toil and care, they became more fully sensible of their crime and with true contrition of heart they, with clasped hands, implored forgiveness; and hence arose the penitential or supplicatory sign, or sign of sorrow.

Now fervent prayer, the grand restorer of true peace of mind and only balm to heal a wounded conscience, first raised a gleam of hope and encouraged them to pursue their daily task with greater cheerfulness: but seized with weariness and pain, the sure effects of constant toil and labour, they were forced to lay their right hands to the region of the heart and their left as a support to the side of their heads; and thus arose the monitorial sign or sign of admonition.

Now their minds being more calm, their toil seemed less severe and, cheered by bright-eyed hope, they clearly saw redemption drawing on and hence arose the last sign, called the fiducial sign or sign of faith and hope.

Q. Why do we use rods in the Chapter?

A. *In Anno Lucis 2513, our most excellent grand master, Moses, tending the flock of Jethro, his father-in-law, at the foot of Mount Sinai, was called by the Almighty and commanded to go down into Egypt and deliver his brethren from their cruel bondage. Moses, then in banishment, greatly hesitated saying Who am I that I should go? The Lord, to encourage him, promised to be with him. Moses, still*

Red Sea.

doubting, begs of Him a sign, to convince him of His power and to confirm His promise. The Lord asked What is in thine hand? Moses answered a rod. The Lord said unto him – cast it on the ground. This done it immediately became a serpent and Moses fled from it. The Lord said unto Moses, Put forth thine hand and take it by the tail; and it became a rod. With this rod he smote the two rocks in the wilderness from whence the waters gushed out. With this rod he divided the waters of the Red Sea and made them to stand as two great heaps. With this rod he wrought his wonders in the Land of Egypt; and therefore to commemorate these singular events and as emblems we make that use of them in our Royal Arch Chapter.

Q   *What definition have you of the banners of the Chapter?*

A   *The banners of the twelve tribes of Israel, which we have for many purposes, especially to commemorate the great wonders which He wrought for the children of Israel during their travels in the wilderness, where they first set up around their encampments and about which each tribe was to pitch its respective standards. The devices thereon were emblematical of their posterity and after ages.*

End of Fifth Section

Commentary

The first point made in this section concerns the double cube, what we know as the altar of incense on the floor of our Chapter. Believe it or not, the construction of a double cube is one of those geometrical problems that has fascinated mathematicians since the ancient Greeks. One could be excused for thinking that to make a double cube one just makes two cubes and fixes them one on top of the other. Not so. The problem is well known outside Freemasonry in things like Kabbalistic magic.

Wikipedia says: *The problem owes its name to a story concerning the citizens of Delos, who consulted the oracle at Delphi in order to learn how to defeat a plague sent by Apollo. According to Plutarch it was the citizens of Delos who consulted the oracle at Delphi, seeking a solution for their internal political problems at the time, which had intensified relationships among the citizens. The oracle responded that they must double the size of the altar to Apollo, which was a regular cube. The answer seemed strange to the Delians and they consulted Plato, who was able to interpret the oracle as the mathematical problem of doubling the volume of a given cube, thus explaining the oracle as the advice of Apollo for the citizens of Delos to occupy themselves with the study of geometry and mathematics in order to calm down their passions.*

According to Plutarch, Plato gave the problem to Eudoxus of Cnidus and Archytas and Menaechmus, who solved the problem using mechanical means, earning a rebuke from Plato for not solving the problem using pure geometry (Plut., Quaestiones convivales, 718ef). This may be why the problem is referred to in the 350s BC by the author of the pseudo-Platonic Sisyphus (dialogue) (388e) as still unsolved. However, another version of the story says that all three found solutions but they were too abstract to be of practical value.[54]

Passing on to the jewel, which we have covered elsewhere, the reference to a Basilidean emblem in relation to agriculture will be strange to most of us. The Basilideans were a sect founded by Basilides of Alexandria in the second century AD and was not dissimilar to the school of Pythagoras at Croton, having three grades – material, intellectual and spiritual – much like the three degrees of Craft Masonry. However, this lecture appears to be critical of Basilidean thought so it need detain us no longer.

Looking at the five signs, we can see distinct similarities to the signs we use to day. The penal sign is known here as the venal sign. The reverential or hailing, penitential or supplicatory and fiducial signs are in many respects similar. The monitorial sign, however, is very different.

Moses by Michaelangelo.

The question about rods is intriguing. The rod, as the lecture says, recalls the incident where God commanded Moses to cast his rod on the ground, when it became a serpent which Moses was instructed to take by the tail, when it became a rod again. There was also Aaron's rod 'which budded, blossomed and yielded almonds all in one night' to be afterwards laid up in the Ark of the Covenant as a token against the rebellious.

But there is a further connotation. The rod, wand or staff of office has been a symbol of authority since the beginning of time. Neville Barker Cryer

---

54 Wikipedia – The Double Cube

points out that operative master architects carried a staff of office and that they were also used in the Church. To this day, in some places both churchwardens carry wands (one with a mite on, which used to be carried by the Vicar's warden, and the other with a crown formerly carried by the people's warden although today both are just called wardens). On special occasions, such as when the bishop visits (carrying his pastoral staff or crozier, which is another kind of wand), these wands are carried. But at one time the vicar had a wand as well. Cryer claims that originally in lodges, the Master and the Wardens had wands, which were derived from the vicar and the churchwardens. After the Union of 1813 when lodges assumed the form they have now instead of everyone sitting round a long table and Deacons appeared, the Wardens' wands passed to the Deacons and the Master's to the DC.

Cryer continues: *As the original Royal Arch ceremony required a brother to be both a Mark Master and an Installed Master it was natural for such a brother to have already received such a wand or staff. This he would have as a 'Harod' or foreman, when he became a Mark Master, or as a ruler of other Excellent Masons when placed in the Chair. At his investiture as a Royal Arch Mason it was recognised that since he had had to take another step to complete this grade of master, he was relieved of his staff at the door of the Chapter and was now having it returned.*

When the candidate is being invested he is also entrusted with a staff of office (wand) which he will always be permitted to bear unless seventy-two of his elders are present.

The Modern Lectures

After 1835 the present concept of Historical, Symbolical and Mystical Lectures emerged and we will now look at these.

1. The Historical Lecture

Until the early years of this century, the Historical Lecture was handicapped by being based on the long discredited chronology of Archbishop Ussher. James Ussher (1581-1656) was Church of Ireland (Anglican) Archbishop of Armagh and Primate of all Ireland between 1625 and 1656. He was basing his chronology on a contention that the creation of the world took place on Sunday, 23 October 4004 BC. This we now know to be false so the whole chronology becomes unreliable.

Other than that, the Historical Lecture traces the history of the Three Original Grand Lodges which we have already covered: the First or Holy Lodge, which was the Tabernacle erected at the foot of Mount Horeb in the wilderness of Sinai by Moses, Aholiab and Bezaleel, the Second or Sacred Lodge in the bosom of Holy Mount Moriah by Solomon, King of Israel, Hiram, King of Tyre and Hiram Abif, the widow's son and finally the Third or Grand and Royal Lodge brought about by Zerubbabel, Prince of the people, Haggai the prophet and Joshua, the son of Josedech, the high priest.

King David.

The term 'bosom of Holy Mount Moriah' requires some explanation. The mount has been considered sacred right back to the time of the creation. It was the site of Enoch's Royal Arch. It was the place where Abraham bound his son, Isaac, to be sacrificed when the ram appeared in the thicket and provided a more acceptable sacrifice. It is also the spot on which Jacob had his dream of the angels of God ascending and descending a ladder to heaven. King David, having conquered the city and made it his own, bought the land on which the Temple was to be built from Araunah, King of the Jebusites, whom he had defeated. When reciting this lecture many Royal Arch Masons get the comma in the wrong place. Araunah was the Jebusite, David was an Israelite. David, the conqueror, could presumably have just confiscated the site but he in fact paid Araunah six hundred shekels for it.

Then we see the reconstruction of the Temple under the Third or Grand and Royal Lodge and its final destruction by the Romans, under Titus in AD 70 (although it had fallen into disrepair before that and been renovated by Herod the Great). Herod's Temple is the one referred to in the New Testament and is described as a wonder of the world. It was built in a manner similar to King Solomon's Temple, using timber from the cedars of Lebanon, floated down the coast and without hammering of metals within the Temple precincts. Herod was extremely wealthy from landholdings, produce and metal rights all over the Near East. So money was no object. History and the Bible record him as a thoroughly nasty character. In fact Peter Ustinov once said that, as a child, he didn't like going to Harrod's department store because he thought that King Herod lived there. This Herod is not the one who dealt with John the Baptist and Jesus. That was Herod Antipas.

We should not however pass over the destruction by Titus without looking a little more closely at just what happened.

Jesus Himself foretold the destruction of Jerusalem:

All that is left of Herod's Temple – The Western Wall.

And when ye shall see Jerusalem compassed with armies, then know that the desolation thereof is nigh. Then let them which are in Judaea flee to the mountains; and let them which are in the midst of it depart out; and let not them that are in the countries enter thereinto. For these be the days of vengeance, that all things which are written may be fulfilled. But woe unto them that are with child, and to them that give suck, in those days! for there shall be great distress in the land, and wrath upon this people. And they shall fall by the edge of the sword, and shall be led away captive into all nations: and Jerusalem shall be trodden down of the Gentiles, until the times of the Gentiles be fulfilled.[55]

Not even that stern warning prepares us for what eventually happened. Briefly, during the reign of the Emperor Nero, Rome lost control in Jerusalem and the city was being controlled by rival Jewish gangs under different warlords. Nero's reign was one of incompetence and great cruelty. He murdered his first wife and his mother and accidentally kicked his pregnant second wife to death. He had fiddled whilst Rome burned in AD 64 and then blamed the fire on the Christians, after which he crucified St.Peter upside down and beheaded St.Paul. A lot of atrocities were committed but, in a curious parallel with today, people did not really get excited about it until the economy got in a mess.

The situation in Jerusalem was chaotic. King Herod Agrippa remained loyal to Rome but against him were ranged the Temple Priests and two major warlord factions – the Zealots and the Sicarii. The Roman Procurator Gessius Florus was sent to restore order and did so with great brutality, charging down Jews who had come to welcome him with cavalry, entering houses and slaughtering the inhabitants and, after his legionaries had run amok in the streets, meting out flagellations and crucifixions. He did restore order but by this time the main body of the Jewish resistance had taken control of the Temple and were holed up there.

King Herod Agrippa and his Queen Berenice begged the Jews to spare the Temple. The king's troops and supporters controlled the upper city of Jerusalem. Jew fought Jew with great ferocity and 12,000 were killed.

Enter Vespasian and his son, Titus. The normal garrison in Jerusalem was 600 men. Titus was sent to Egypt and raised an army of 60,000 which

---

55 St.Luke's Gospel chapter 21 vv 21–24

proceeded to reconquer Judea and finally finished up in front of Jerusalem.

Nero then committed suicide in AD 68. This moved things along because, after three weak emperors had been got out of the way, the legions in Judea and Egypt declared for Vespasian as their new Emperor. Titus entered Jerusalem and seized the city, which was still being fought over by two major warlords – John of Gischala and Simon ben Giora – who were slugging it out for control of the Temple and the city. John invited in a barbarous race called the Idumeans from south of Jerusalem who attacked the Inner Temple and even the Holy of Holies. All that remained was for Titus to march in and finish the job. An arch (ironically) in Rome still commemorates Titus' victory.[56]

Titus' Triumphal Arch in Rome, commemorating his victory over the Jews.

But the story does not quite end there. About 1,000 refugees from Jerusalem overcame a small Roman garrison and took control of the fortress of Masada (which in Hebrew means fortress) about 87 miles from Jerusalem. Masada is perched on top of a rock shaped like the prow of a ship and had been built by Herod in around AD 40 as a summer palace. The Roman General, Lucius Flavius Silva, incensed by the uprising, pursued them and laid siege to the rock, constructing a ramp so that he could scale the rock and break down the gates with battering rams.[57]

Inside the Jews, realising that they could not withstand a Roman army, committed mass suicide with each man killing his wife and children. Ten men were selected to oversee the killing of 960 people and the only survivors were those who had hidden themselves. General Silva recorded that he had won 'A rock in the middle of a wasteland, on the shores of a poisoned sea' (the Dead Sea).

The Fortress of Masada.

After returning to Rome in triumph, Titus succeeded his father, Vespasian, as emperor but only reigned for two years before his early death, which the Jews saw as God's punishment.

To this day the memory of Masada remains deeply ingrained upon the Jewish psyche.

Finally we conclude the Historical Lecture by drawing a comparison between the officers of a Royal Arch Chapter and the Grand Originals in Jerusalem.

56 Simon Sebag Montefiore – *Jerusalem: the Biography* – Phoenix, 2011
57 Mira Bar-Hillel – *The Stunning Story of Masada* – Times article

2. The Symbolical Lecture

This lecture attempts to explain and expound some, if not all, of the symbolism of what we find before us when we sit in a Royal Arch Chapter. It starts off by explaining the form of a Chapter – approaching a true Catenarian arch, with the Three Principals forming the keystone and two contiguous arch stones, the Sojourners the base and the Scribes and the rest of the Companions figure as the columns of the arch. So we are forming a representation of the sacred arch in which the true name of God was deposited, but also reminding ourselves that the arch only stays together if all the pieces are connected and compressed together and hence the need for inviolable secrecy.

We then go on to look at the lights, describing how by their intersections they form a given number of triangles which when reduced to their amount in right angles will be found to correspond with the mysterious Triple Tau, the Companion's jewel and the four elements and the sphere of the Universe. These we have covered elsewhere.

The lecture also discusses the ribbon worn by the Companions, the ensigns on the staves and the four principal banners, the bearings on the sceptres, the Bible, square and compasses, the sword and trowel and the pick-axe, crowbar and shovel. Again we have already considered the symbolism of these items.

We should note that this lecture makes reference to the concept of masons working with trowel in hand and sword by their side, which we have also covered elsewhere.

Lt.-Cdr. C. R. Manasseh describes the Symbolical Lecture in the following terms:

The second lecture is the Symbolical Lecture and, in a way, can be compared to the giving of the working tools in the three Craft degrees, all rolled into one except that the tools and ornaments described are different. The Symbolical Lecture is in fact a transposition in the life hereafter of the lectures on the working tools of this life as given in the Craft degrees. It therefore has a symbolism all of its own and aims, in my opinion, to raise the candidate's feelings to his Higher Feeling, his emotions to his Higher Emotion.

That is a little difficult to follow because the Craft working tool Lectures are about adapting the tools of an operative mason to our morals, whilst the Royal Arch working tools (the sword, trowel, etc.) are given in an historical context, but what Manasseh says next is interesting:

The second lecture, delivered by H., the Symbolical Lecture is again self evident. It goes through all the ornaments of the Chapter, movable and immovable, and proceeds to expound on their symbolism. Once again, it is interesting to note that 'Mysticism', as defined by the dictionary, underlies the main theme of this lecture as well, since a major proportion of it dwells on the symbolism of the Divinity. In the greater part of the text, this subject is only glossed over: this lecture merely makes reference to 'The Sacred Word', yet it is the forerunner of the Mystical Lecture, not only in that it is a preface to it, but also in that it can be interpreted as pointing to at least seven Schools of mystical revelations, spread over four different sections of the lecture:

1. The prehistoric cave mysticism (Cromagnon and others), and the Eleusinian mysticism of Germination (i.e. the mysteries of Nature), as hinted by the Vault and its sacred contents.

2. Kabbalistic mysticism, as evident in the arrangements of the Lights, and the Seal of Solomon in the Jewel worn by the companions.

3. Pythagorean and Neo-Platonic mysticism, both in the brief reference to the five Platonic Bodies and in the more detailed explanation of the triangulations of the Lights and the geometry of the Triple Tau and the Jewel.

4. The two famous mysticisms which in fact probably belong to one and the same School, because they are so strikingly similar that they have the appearance of being identical, i.e. the Hebraic mysticism of the Merkabah vision of Ezekiel (Ezekiel, chapter 1); and the Christian mysticism of the Apocalyptic vision of St. John (Revelation, chapter 4). Both have the same mystical vision of the Shekinah Glory or Divine Immanence riding in an incandescent chariot of flames, drawn by the same four Angelic Beasts: the Man, the Lion, the Ox and the Eagle (Ezekiel i, 10 and Revelation iv, 7), the emblems of the Patriarchal Blessing, which were later borne on the standards of the four leading tribes who ruled respectively over the South, East, West and North columns in marching, camping or fighting order, during the Exodus (Numbers, chapter 2)[58].

3. Mystical Lecture

In looking at the Mystical Lecture we are considering something altogether deeper than the previous two. The present permissive alternative versions of the lecture in both the Complete and Aldersgate workings no longer include the signs, which themselves have permissive alternative versions which must be given, together with the lecture itself when a candidate is exalted.

We are first told that a vast number of Masons were employed at the building of King Solomon's Temple and their names were found engraved in different parts of the building. The names of the Three Grand Masters were nowhere to be found. This is a little confusing because the names of the workmen would be recorded, presumably by their Masons' marks in order that they might get paid. The names of the Three Grand Masters were deposited in the sacred vault in order to hand those names and their respective insignia down to posterity, in other words for a totally different purpose.

---

58 Lt.-Cdr. C. R. Manasseh – *The Mysticism of the Royal Arch*

We then re-visit the story of how the Sojourners found the sacred name of God in the vault and conceived it to be that which they had always been forbidden to know – the Sacred Name of God. This they found on top of the white double cube on a plate of gold within a triangle and a circle. Then, underneath, they find the initials of the Three Grand Masters and the Triple Tau, the significance of which we have already looked at. What we see when restored to light at our Exaltation is presumably what the legend is telling us that the Sojourner saw when he discovered the vault, but in addition we see the companions tilting their banners in imitation of the arches leading to the place where the sacred name was and the Principals holding their sceptres in a triangle.

The closing words of the lecture are crucially important. It used to say:

It has virtue for its aim and the glory of God for its object, and the eternal welfare of man is considered in every part, point and letter of its ineffable mysteries. Suffice it to say, it is founded on the Sacred Name of God, who was from all beginning, is now, and will remain One and the same for ever, the Being alone existing in and from Himself in all actual perfection, original in His essence.

The wording has now changed so that we no longer talk of ineffable mysteries. But what does ineffable mean? The dictionary definition is: *incapable of being expressed or described in words; inexpressible or not to be spoken because of its sacredness; unutterable: the ineffable name of the deity.* In other words, the Degree is founded on the Sacred Name of God which could, and can, only be pronounced under defined, restricted circumstances.

The concluding paragraph now says: *This Supreme Degree inspires its members with the most exalted ideas of God and leads to the exercise of the purest and most sublime piety; a reverence for the incomprehensible J———h, the Eternal Ruler of the Universe, the elemental life and primordial source of all its principles, the very spring and fount of all its virtues.*

A couple of phrases there need a little explanation. For instance *The Elemental Life* – what is that about? The modern theory is that there are actually four primary Elemental Kingdoms, represented as Fire, Air, Water and Earth. Within these four kingdoms there exists an order of Nature spirits that govern and control the four forces that manifest everything we cannot see. Whether the phrase meant the same to the 19th century compilers of our ritual, I know not, although the Comte de Saint-Germain who first seems to have propounded the theory of spirits manipulating the elements lived in the 18th century.

The *primordial source of all its principles and the very spring and fount of all its virtues* are possibly easier to understand. They are simply saying that God was the originator of all things.

In passing, we may note that there is more than one meaning of

'Word'. The opening of St. John's Gospel with the words 'In the beginning was the Word and the Word was with God and the Word was God' is telling us that Jesus Christ as part of the Holy Trinity had always existed. It is not my purpose to get too theological because the Royal Arch is open to non-Christians but it interesting to note the following extract from the ritual of the Royal Order of Scotland:

> Q. *Whom did you meet with in that Middle Chamber?*
> A. *Three wise men.*
> Q. *How did they dispose of you?*
> A. *They led me to the Cabinet of Wisdom*
> Q. *What is meant by the Cabinet of Wisdom?*
> A. *An ox's stall.*
> Q. *Whom did you meet with in this same Cabinet of Wisdom?*
> A. *A most glorious Brother, his most Holy Spouse and the ever-blessed Word.*

4. The Signs

The signs of the Degree must always be explained whenever a candidate is exalted. We can only discuss them in outline here but it is worth noting that the only biblical figure referred to now is Moses. Adam and his original sin were referred to in earlier versions of the ritual. There are five signs which correspond in number to the Five Points of Fellowship and of course we recall that the number five was key in early Royal Arch ceremonies. Only one of these signs can be accurately described as a 'working sign' and even the use of that has now been very much reduced. The Rev. F. De P. Castells felt that all these signs were connected with Adam and his fall and that their origin was firstly from when the Royal Arch was worked as part of the Third Degree and then also from the ceremony of Passing of the Veils.[59]

The signs differ in other parts of the world – certainly those illustrated in *Duncan's Ritual of Freemasonry* – in common use in the United States, are with one exception strange to us. Of course we have to remember that when the Chapter of Promulgation was warranted in 1835 for six months to standardise the ritual in accordance with the wishes of HRH The Duke of Sussex, a lot of not standardisation, but sanitisation, occurred (as it did in the Craft some years earlier) whereby a lot of what was known before the Union was swept away so that signs exported to other parts of the world are no longer known to us.

An alternative explanation of the signs, associating it with the Degree rather than anything else, is as follows:

---

59 Rev F. De P. Castells – *Historical Analysis of the Holy Royal Arch Ritual* (1929)

The First or P. S. refers to the Sojourner guarding his eyes from the intensity of the sun's rays, when their reflection shone so brilliantly on the gold plate found on the pedestal.

The Second is the sign of Salute, called also the Reverential, and refers to the second ascent from the vault. Tradition informs us that the Sojourner, on bringing up the scroll from the vault, bound his two companions to secrecy by the P. S., he himself being obliged to use his left hand, as his right was occupied with the Roll.

The Third is the Penitential or Supplicatory sign given in allusion to the thankfulness of the chiefs of the Sanhedrin when they recovered the long lost Book of the Law.

The Fourth is the Monitorial or sign of Suffering, given in allusion to the descent of the Sojourner into the vault,

The Fifth, called the Fiducial, sign is made in allusion to the Sojourner prostrating

Companion's Jewel

himself before the pedestal when he discovered what it was.

The Grand sign refers to the opening of the arches by the removal of the three stones, which stones are typified by the three Principals Z. H. and J. The three halts in giving it, and the three arches formed by the three Ps. allude to the three descents of the Sojourners before they discovered the mysterious triangle.[60]

Some of these explanations sound reasonably plausible. We do not use the Grand Sign in England.

5. The Explanation of the Companion's Jewel

This lecture, of all the Royal Arch lectures, is probably the least heard because of its length and complexity and the difficulty of finding anyone with the ability (or the time) to commit it to memory. The latest version of the Complete Workings has now omitted it altogether but some years ago I spent an entire summer learning it, only to find my Companions' eyes glazing over when I delivered it in Chapter! At least I can say I have done it and they can say they have heard it!

Of all the versions of the lecture, the Aldersgate one is certainly the most user-friendly. It does its best to use everyday language throughout and avoids complex Platonic geometry as much as possible.

We have, however, to be aware of the symbolism of the two intersecting triangles right at the centre of the jewel. One points upwards and this represents God; the other goes downwards and this is mankind. They have also been expressed as heaven and earth and the spiritual and material worlds. In alchemy, this six-pointed triangle or hexalpha symbolised the four elements and the sphere of the Universe, as they do with us. We have already seen that the angles in the jewel, when reduced to their amount in right-angles are equal to the Five Regular Platonic Bodies, which also

---

60   From an unknown American source

correspond with the four elements and sphere. A worthy Australian Companion associates the jewel with the Dionysian Artificers:

> Legend or myth has it that the Dionysian Artificers were employed by Solomon and Hiram, King of Tyre in the building of Solomon's temple. It seems certain that they built the Temple of Diana at Ephesus, and it seems rather well accepted that they spread their craftsmanship through the Mediterranean littoral.

> The Dionysiac craft spread through the ancient empire states of Egypt, the Near East, and eventually with the rise of the Roman Empire reached England. They regarded temple architecture as possessing symmetry and proportion. They perfected the architecture for spans, lintels, arches and domes. Certain temples were initially columned by Doric columns. Corinthian columns were allotted to other special temples while the Ionic columns are believed by some authorities to have been founded upon astronomical principles. One of the legends concerning the origins of the Ionic column tells the story of the principal architect of the day in Athens was searching for inspiration for a new style relate to the Acropolis, it is said was laid out to assimilate the shape of the famous asterism known as the Pleiades, or Seven Sisters.

> Hall believes that the Dionysian tradition continued into the mediaeval times in Europe, and constructed the early types of religious architecture such as abbeys and churches. He also attributes the Roman Collegia were derived from the Dionysians. He believes that the chequered pavement in Masonic Lodges originates with the Dionysians, who in mediaeval times called themselves as the Sons of Solomon, motified by the interlaced triangles. There is even a suggestion that the Knights Templar were associated with them. In transmitting the tradition to Freemasonry, the Dionysians passed the traditions of the secrets of symbolic architecture to Freemasonry. With them passed on the symbols now associated with Freemasonry – the chief symbolism being that of the unfinished temple of civilisation. They also used the symbolisms of the rough and perfect ashlars.[61] The Triple Tau in the centre bottom of the jewel was not adopted until the reforms of 1835 (although reference is made to it in Carlile's exposure of 1825 and much further back as we shall see in a moment), before which the motif took the form of a T over an H, standing for *Templum Hierosolyma* or Temple at Jerusalem. The Tau has of course been said also to represent the three steps taken by an Entered Apprentice before his obligation, the position of the feet when brought together and also the levels on a Master's apron. Even though these last are more connected with the Craft we ought to be aware of them. The reason for this is that what we started with three knocks on the door in the Degree of Entered Apprentice, symbolizing *'Ask and ye shall receive, seek and ye shall find and knock and it will be open to you'*, culminates in the centre piece of the

---

61 R. E. Comp. Arthur A. Page, P.G.J., Grand Lecturer, S.G.R.A.C. Queensland – *Symbolism of the Holy Royal Arch Jewel - the Chequered Pavement*

jewel – the Triple Tau. This Triple Tau is first encountered in a water-clock exhibited in the Provincial Museum in Durham. It is surprising to find the Triple Tau amongst the many other Masonic emblems displayed on the clock but we must remember that this is an area in which Operative Masonry predominated and the Tau was known to the building trade as the 'Builder's Trinity' or the 'Holy Jesus'.[62]

We have discussed the mottoes on the jewel earlier but the shape of the triangles and their relationships with the four elements and the intersecting lights are what we must now look at.

Four equal and equilateral (all sides having the same length) triangles are formed by the intersection of the six lights. This was said in the days of the Antients' Grand Lodge to symbolise the four divisions of Masonry – Entered Apprentice, Fellowcraft, Master Mason and Royal Arch. We can see this in Figure 1.

Next we look at the pentagram containing five triangles, in Figure 2 symbolizing the four elements – Earth, Fire, Air and Water – and also the sphere of the universe.

Figure 3 shows the triangles created by the arrangement of the six lights which we see placed around our double-cube altar.

This relates the positions of the lights to the mysterious Triple Tau because the angles of a triangle add up to 180 degrees (or two right angles) in total so that triangles a,b,c and d total four lots of 180 degrees or eight right angles corresponding to the number of right angles in the Triple Tau. It could also be noted that four lots of 180 degrees is equal to two lots of 360 degrees which is two circles as depicted on the Royal Arch jewel (the inner and the outer).

Going back to the four elements and the sphere of the Universe (or as we know them the Five Regular Platonic Bodies) we note that their amount in right angles is as follows:

Using the Tau as a key it is possible to resolve the triangles created on the jewel into an equivalent number of equilateral triangles having the sum of their angles numerically equivalent to 8, 16, 24, 40 and 72 right angles, representing respectively:

Fire: the Tetrahedron, having 4 equal and equilateral triangles with the equivalent of 8 right angles and one triple Tau.

Air: the Octahedron, having 8 equal and equilateral triangles with the equivalent of 16 right angles and two triple Taus.

Earth: the Cube, having 6 equal squares with 24 right angles and three triple Taus.

Water: the Icosahedron, having 20 equal and equilateral triangles with the equivalent of

Fig 1

Fig 2

Fig 3

---

62 Aldersgate Ritual The Jewel of the Order

40 right angles and five Triple Taus.

Sphere of the Universe: the Dodecahedron, having 12 equal and equilateral pentagons with the equivalent of 72 right angles and nine triple Taus.[63]

Fig 4

This is illustrated by Figure 4. If you look at the intersections of the two larger triangles ABC and DEF with the smaller triangle GHI in the centre (without getting too Platonic or too mathematical) you will see how the number of right angles (remember two to every triangle) adds up to equate to the Platonic bodies above.

The explanation of Figure 5, as it used to be given in Sussex, Complete and other rituals is extremely complex, nay mind-blowing to the layman. Kirk McNulty thought that it derived from the Neo-Platonic thought which was in vogue at the time our rituals were first produced, showing that *'the Deity wills itself into existence as Divinity, Soul, Spirit, Materiality and the physical universe'*.[64] We remember from the Mystical Lecture *'the Being alone existing in and from Itself, in actual perfection, original in His essence'*. In other words God created Himself because without Him there was nothing.

Fig 5

For that reason, although the triangle may have symbolised the Holy Trinity in former times, it has also always symbolised the three attributes of God – Omnipotence, Omniscience and Omnipresence. Christopher Powell also points out that the erect triangle (ABC) is a symbol of God in His Justice whilst the downward one (DEF) signifies God in His mercy.[65]

6. The Stone of Foundation

The following treatise forms part of an address given by Bro John A. Lodor before the State Grand Lodge of Alabama in December 1861. I have included it because it puts an entirely new slant on the cubic stone in the middle of our Chapters and offers a lot of other symbolism.

The Stone of Foundation constitutes one of the most important and abstruse of all the symbols of Freemasonry. It is referred to in numerous legends and traditions, not only of the Freemasons, but also Jewish and Moslem ones. Some of them are deeply interesting in their allegorical signification.

The Stone of Foundation is, properly speaking, a symbol of the higher degrees. It makes its first appearance in the Royal Arch, and forms, indeed, the most important symbol of that degree. But it is so intimately connected, in its legendary history, with the construction of the Solomonic temple, that it must be considered as a part of Ancient Craft Masonry,

---

63 E.Comp. A.D. Matthews PPDepGSwdB Camberley Lodge Lectures

64 W. Kirk McNulty – *Neo-Platonism and the Royal Arch Triple Tau*

65 Christopher Powell – *The Royal Arch Jewel - an explanation* – AQC123 2010

although he who confines the range of his investigations to the first three degrees, will have no means, within that narrow limit, of properly appreciating the symbolism of the Stone of Foundation.

As preliminary to the inquiry which is about to be instituted, it is necessary to distinguish the Stone of Foundation, both in its symbolism and in its legendary history, from other stones which play an important part in the Masonic ritual, but which are entirely distinct from it. Such are the *corner-stone*, which was always placed in the north-east corner of the building about to be erected, and to which such a beautiful reference is made in the ceremonies of the first degree; or the keystone, which constitutes an interesting part of the Mark Master's degree; or, lastly, the *cape-stone*, upon which all the ritual of the Most Excellent Master's degree is founded. These are all, in their proper places, highly interesting and instructive symbols, but have no connection whatever with the Stone of Foundation or its symbolism. Nor, although the Stone of Foundation is said, for peculiar reasons, to have been of a cubical form, must it be confounded with that stone called by the continental Masons the *cubical stone* – the *pierre cubique* of the French, and the *cubik stein* of the German Masons, but which in the English system is known as the *perfect ashlar*.

The Stone of Foundation has a legendary history and a symbolic signification which are peculiar to itself, and which differ from the history and meaning which belong to these other stones.

Let us first define this Masonic Stone of Foundation, then collate the legends which refer to it, and afterwards investigate its significance as a symbol. To the Mason who takes a pleasure in the study of the mysteries of his institution, the investigation cannot fail to be interesting, if it is conducted with any ability.

The Stone of Foundation is supposed, by the theory which establishes it, to have been a stone placed at one time within the foundations of the temple of Solomon, and afterwards, during the building of the second temple, transported to the Holy of Holies. It was in form a perfect cube, and had inscribed upon its upper face, within a delta or triangle, the sacred tetragrammaton, or ineffable name of God. Oliver, speaking with the solemnity of an historian, says that Solomon thought that he had rendered the house of God worthy, so far as human adornment could effect, for the dwelling of God, 'when he had placed the celebrated Stone of Foundation, on which the sacred name was mystically engraven, with solemn ceremonies, in that sacred depository on Mount Moriah, along with the foundations of Dan and Asher, the centre of the Most Holy Place, where the ark was overshadowed by the shekinah of God.' The Hebrew Talmudists, who thought as much of this stone, and had as many legends concerning it as the masonic Talmudists, called it *eben shatijah* or 'Stone of Foundation,' because, as they said, it had been laid by Jehovah as the foundation of the world; and hence the apocryphal book of Enoch speaks of the 'stone which supports the corners of the earth.'

This idea of a foundation stone of the world was most probably derived from that magnificent passage of the book of Job, in which the Almighty demands of the afflicted patriarch:

'Where wast thou, when I laid the foundation of the earth? Declare, since thou hast such knowledge! Who fixed its dimensions, since thou knowest? Or who stretched out the line upon it? Upon what were its foundations fixed? And who laid its corner-stone, When the morning stars sang together, And all the sons of God shouted for joy?'

Noyes, whose beautiful translation I have adopted as not materially differing from the common version, but which is far more poetical and more in the strain of the original, thus explains the allusions to the foundation-stone: 'It was the custom to celebrate the laying of the corner-stone of an important building with music, songs, shouting, &c. Hence the morning stars are represented as celebrating the laying of the corner-stone of the earth.'

Upon this meagre statement have been accumulated more traditions than appertain to any other masonic symbol. The Rabbis, as has already been intimated, divide the glory of these apocryphal histories with the Masons; indeed, there is good reason for a suspicion that nearly all the Masonic legends owe their first existence to the imaginative genius of the writers of the Jewish Talmud. But there is this difference between the Hebrew and the masonic traditions, that the Talmudic scholar recited them as truthful histories, and swallowed, in one gulp of faith, all their impossibilities and anachronisms, while the Masonic student has received them as allegories, whose value is not in the facts, but in the sentiments which they convey.

With this understanding of their meaning, let us proceed to a collation of these legends.

In that blasphemous work, the *'Toldoth Jeshu'* or *Life of Jesus*, written, it is supposed, in the 13th or 14th century, we find the following account of this wonderful stone:

'At that time [the time of Jesus] *there was in the House of the Sanctuary [that is, the temple] a Stone of Foundation, which is the very stone that our father Jacob anointed with oil, as it is described in the twenty-eighth chapter of the book of Genesis. On that stone the letters of the tetragrammaton were inscribed, and whosoever of the*

Israelites should learn that name would be able to master the world. To prevent, therefore, any one from learning these letters, two iron dogs were placed upon two columns in front of the Sanctuary. If any person, having acquired the knowledge of these letters, desired to depart from the Sanctuary, the barking of the dogs, by magical power, inspired so much fear, that he suddenly forgot what he had acquired.'

There is also the following passage:

'At that time there was in the temple the ineffable name of God, inscribed upon the Stone of Foundation. For when King David was digging the foundation for the temple, he found in the depths of the excavation a certain stone, on which the name of God was inscribed. This stone he removed, and deposited it in the Holy of Holies.'

The Masonic legends of the Stone of Foundation, based on these and other rabbinical reveries, are of the most extraordinary character, if they are to be viewed as histories, but readily reconcilable with sound sense, if looked at only in the light of allegories. They present an uninterrupted succession of events, in which the Stone of Foundation takes a prominent part, from Adam to Solomon, and from Solomon to Zerubbabel.

Thus the first of these legends, in order of time, relates that the Stone of Foundation was possessed by Adam while in the garden of Eden; that he used it as an altar, and so reverenced it, that, on his expulsion from Paradise, he carried it with him into the world in which he and his descendants were afterwards to earn their bread by the sweat of their brow.

Another legend informs us that from Adam the Stone of Foundation descended to Seth. From Seth it passed by regular succession to Noah, who took it with him into the ark, and after the subsidence of the deluge, made on it his first thank-offering. Noah left it on Mount Ararat, where it was subsequently found by Abraham, who removed it, and consequently used it as an altar of sacrifice. His grandson Jacob took it with him when he fled to his uncle Laban in Mesopotamia, and used it as a pillow when, in the vicinity of Luz, he had his celebrated vision.

Here there is a sudden interruption in the legendary history of the stone, and we have no means of conjecturing how it passed from the possession of Jacob into that of Solomon. Moses, it is true, is said to have taken it with him out of Egypt at the time of the exodus, and thus it may have finally reached Jerusalem. Dr. Adam Clarke repeats what he very properly calls 'a foolish tradition,' that the stone on which Jacob rested his head was afterwards brought to Jerusalem, thence carried after a long lapse of time to Spain, from Spain to Ireland, and from Ireland to Scotland, where it was used as a seat on which the kings of Scotland sat to be crowned. Edward I., we know, brought a stone, to which this legend is attached, from Scotland to Westminster Abbey, where, under the name of

Jacob's Pillow, it still remains, and is always placed under the chair upon which the British sovereign sits to be crowned, because there is an old distich which declares that wherever this stone is found the Scottish kings shall reign. But this Scottish tradition would take the Stone of Foundation away from all its masonic connections, and therefore it is rejected as a Masonic legend.

The legends just related are in many respects contradictory and unsatisfactory, and another series, equally as old, are now very generally adopted by Masonic scholars, as much better suited to the symbolism by which all these legends are explained.

This series of legends commences with the patriarch Enoch, who is supposed to have been the first consecrator of the Stone of Foundation. The legend of Enoch is so interesting and important in Masonic science as to excuse something more than a brief reference to the incidents which it details.

The legend in full is as follows: Enoch, under the inspiration of the Most High, and in obedience to the instructions which he had received in a vision, built a temple under ground on Mount Moriah, and dedicated it to God. His son, Methuselah, constructed the building, although he was not acquainted with his father's motives for the erection. This temple consisted of nine vaults, situated perpendicularly beneath each other, and communicating by apertures left in each vault.

Enoch then caused a triangular plate of gold to be made, each side of which was a cubit long; he enriched it with the most precious stones, and encrusted the plate upon a stone of agate of the same form. On the plate he engraved the true name of God, or the tetragrammaton, and placing it on a cubical stone, known thereafter as the Stone of Foundation, he deposited the whole within the lowest arch.

When this subterranean building was completed, he made a door of stone, and attaching to it a ring of iron, by which it might be occasionally raised, he placed it over the opening of the uppermost arch, and so covered it that the aperture could not be discovered. Enoch himself was not permitted to enter it but once a year, and after the days of Enoch, Methuselah, and Lamech, and the destruction of the world by the deluge, all knowledge of the vault or subterranean temple, and of the Stone of Foundation, with the sacred and ineffable name inscribed upon it, was lost for ages to the world.

At the building of the first temple of Jerusalem, the Stone of Foundation again makes its appearance. Reference has already been made to the Jewish tradition that David, when digging the foundations of the temple, found in the excavation which he was making a certain stone, on which the ineffable name of God was inscribed, and which stone he is said to have removed and deposited in the Holy of Holies. That King David laid the foundations of the temple upon which the superstructure was subsequently erected by Solomon, is a favourite theory of the legend-mongers of the Talmud.

The Masonic tradition is substantially the same as the Jewish, but it substitutes Solomon for David, thereby giving a greater air of probability to the narrative; and it supposes that the stone thus discovered by Solomon was the identical one that had been deposited in his secret vault by Enoch. This Stone of Foundation, the tradition states, was subsequently removed by King Solomon, and, for wise purposes, deposited in a secret and safer place.

In this the Masonic tradition again agrees with the Jewish, for we find in the third chapter of the Treatise on the Temple written by the celebrated Maimonides, the following narrative:

'There was a stone in the Holy of Holies, on its west side, on which was placed the Ark of the Covenant, and before it the pot of manna and Aaron's rod. But when Solomon had built the temple, and foresaw that it was, at some future time, to be destroyed, he constructed a deep and winding vault under ground, for the purpose of concealing the ark, wherein Josiah afterwards, as we learn in the Second Book of Chronicles, xxxv. 3, deposited it, with the pot of manna, the rod of Aaron, and the oil of anointing.'

There is much controversy as to the question of the existence of any ark in the second temple. Some of the Jewish writers assert that a new one was made; others, that the old one was found where it had been concealed by Solomon; and others again contend that there was no ark at all in the temple of Zerubbabel, but that its place was supplied by the Stone of Foundation on which it had originally rested.

Royal Arch Masons well know how all these traditions are sought to be reconciled by the masonic legend, in which the substitute ark and the Stone of Foundation play so important a part.

In the thirteenth degree of the Ancient and Accepted Rite, the Stone of Foundation is conspicuous as the resting-place of the sacred delta.

In the Royal Arch and Select Master's degrees of the Americanized York Rite, the Stone of Foundation constitutes the most important part of the ritual. In both of these it is the receptacle of the ark, on which the ineffable name is inscribed.

Lee, in his Temple of Solomon, has devoted a chapter to this Stone of Foundation, and thus recapitulates the Talmudic and Rabbinical traditions on the subject:

'Vain and futile are the feverish dreams of the ancient Rabbis concerning the Foundation Stone of the temple. Some assert that God placed this stone in the centre of the world, for a future basis and settled consistency for the earth to rest upon. Others *held this stone to be the first matter, out of which all the beautiful visible beings of the world have been hewn forth and produced to light. Others relate that this was the very same stone laid by Jacob for a pillow under his head, in that night when he dreamed of an angelic vision at Bethel, and afterwards anointed and consecrated it to God. Which when Solomon had found he durst not but lay it sure, as the principal foundation stone of the temple. Nay, they say further, he caused to be engraved upon it the tetragrammaton, or the ineffable name of Jehovah.'*

It will be seen that the Masonic traditions on the subject of the Stone of Foundation do not differ very materially from these Rabbinical ones, although they give a few additional circumstances.

In the Masonic legend, the Foundation Stone first makes its appearance, as I have already said, in the days of Enoch, who placed it in the bowels of Mount Moriah. There it was subsequently discovered by King Solomon, who deposited it in a crypt of the first temple, where it remained concealed until the foundations of the second temple were laid, when it was discovered and removed to the Holy of Holies. But the most important point of the legend of the Stone of Foundation is its intimate and constant connection with the tetragrammaton, or ineffable name. It is this name, inscribed upon it, within the sacred and symbolic delta, that gives to the stone all its Masonic value and significance. It is upon this fact that it was so inscribed, that its whole symbolism depends.

Looking at these traditions in anything like the light of historical narratives, we are compelled to consider them, to use the plain language of Lee, 'but as so many idle and absurd conceits'. We must go behind the legend, viewing it only as an allegory, and study its symbolism.

The symbolism of the Foundation Stone of Masonry is therefore the next subject of investigation.

In approaching this, the most abstruse, and one of the most important, symbols of the Order, we are at once impressed with its apparent connection with the ancient doctrine of stone worship. Some brief consideration of this species of religious culture is therefore necessary for a proper understanding of the real symbolism of the Stone of Foundation.

Thus, then, the following facts have been established, but not precisely in this order: First, that there was a very general prevalence among the earliest nations of antiquity of the worship of stones as the representatives of Deity; secondly, that in almost every ancient temple there was a legend of a sacred or mystical stone; thirdly, that this legend is found in the Masonic system; and lastly, that the mystical stone there has received the name of the 'Stone of Foundation'.

Now, as in all the other systems the stone is admitted to be symbolic, and the tradition connected with it mystical, we are compelled to assume the same predicates of the masonic stone. It, too, is symbolic, and its legend a myth or an allegory.

Of the fable, myth, or allegory, Bailly has said that, 'subordinate to history and philosophy, it only deceives that it may the better instruct us. Faithful in preserving the realities which are confided to it, it covers with its seductive envelope the lessons of the one and the truths of the other.' It is from this standpoint that we are to view the allegory of the Stone of Foundation, as developed in one of the most interesting and important symbols of Masonry.

The fact that the mystical stone in all the ancient religions was a symbol of the Deity, leads us necessarily to the conclusion that the Stone of Foundation was also a symbol of Deity. And this symbolic idea is strengthened by the tetragrammaton, or sacred name of God, that was inscribed upon it. This ineffable name sanctifies the stone upon which it is engraved as the symbol of the Grand Architect. It takes from it its heathen signification as an idol, and consecrates it to the worship of the true God.

The predominant idea of the Deity, in the Masonic system, connects him with his creative and formative power. God is, to the Freemason, *Al Gabil*, as the Arabians called him, that is, *The Builder*; or, as expressed in his Masonic title, the G.A.O.T.U. Now, it is evident that no symbol could so appropriately suit him in this character as the Stone of Foundation, upon which he is allegorically supposed to have erected his world. Such a symbol closely connects the creative work of God, as a pattern and exemplar, with the workman's erection of his temporal building on a similar foundation stone.

But this Masonic idea is still further to be extended. The great object of all Masonic labour is *divine truth*. The search for the *lost word* is the search for truth. But divine truth is a term synonymous with God. The ineffable name is a symbol of truth, because God, and God alone, is truth. It is properly a scriptural idea. The Book of Psalms abounds with this sentiment. Thus it is said that the truth of the Lord 'reacheth unto the clouds,' and that 'his truth endureth unto all generations'. If, then, God is truth, and the Stone of Foundation is the masonic symbol of God, it follows that it must also be the symbol of divine truth.

When we have arrived at this point in our speculations, we are ready to show how all the myths and legends of the Stone of Foundation may be rationally explained as parts of that beautiful 'science of morality, veiled in allegory and illustrated by symbols,' which is the acknowledged definition of Freemasonry.

In the Masonic system there are two temples; the first temple, in which the degrees of Ancient Craft Masonry are concerned, and the second temple, with which the higher degrees, and especially the Royal Arch, are related. The first temple is symbolic of the present life; the second temple is symbolic of the life to come. The first temple, the present life, must be destroyed; on its foundations the second temple, the life eternal, must be built.

But the mystical stone was placed by King Solomon in the foundations of the first temple. That is to say, the first temple of our present life must be built on the sure foundation of divine truth, 'for other foundation can no man lay'.

But although the present life is necessarily built upon the foundation of truth, yet we never thoroughly attain it in this sublunary sphere. The Foundation Stone is concealed in the first temple, and the Master Mason knows it not. He has not the true word. He receives only a substitute.

But in the second temple of the future life, we have passed from the grave, which had been the end of our labours in the first. We have removed the rubbish, and have found that Stone of Foundation which had been hitherto concealed from our eyes. We now throw aside the substitute for truth which had contented us in the former temple, and the brilliant effulgence of the tetragrammaton and the Stone of Foundation are discovered, and thenceforth we are the possessors of the true word – of divine truth. And in this way, the Stone of Foundation, or divine truth, concealed in the first temple, but discovered and brought to light in the second, will explain that passage of the apostle, 'For now we see through a glass darkly, but then face to face: now I know in part; but then shall I know even as also I am known.'

And so, the result of this inquiry is, that the Masonic Stone of Foundation is a symbol of divine truth, upon which all Speculative Masonry is built, and the legends and traditions which refer to it are intended to describe, in an allegorical way, the progress of truth in the soul, the search for which is a Mason's labour, and the discovery of which is his reward.

CHAPTER 10

The Installation of the Principals

Every year most Chapters install Three Principals. The order in which this is done, of course, varies with the ritual being used. Complete, Metropolitan and Sussex workings obligate the Third then the Second and finally the First Principal and then, after the Companions below the rank of First Principal have retired, install the three of them in reverse order of Z, H and finally J. Aldersgate does it differently: the obligations are in the order of J, H and Z as before but then J is installed and retires, then H is installed and retires and finally Z is installed.

Principals are designated as Excellent Companions and it is worth noting that a Third Principal elect becomes an Ex.Comp (or E.Comp) as soon as he is elected and should change his regalia accordingly – this is obviously different from the situation in the Craft. The First Principal has the title Most Excellent attached to his office but not to his name. In other words, he is MEZ of Puddlecoombe Chapter but he remains simply Excellent Companion Bloggs.

It is of course possible that circumstances will oblige one, two or even all three Principals to remain in office for a second year (but no longer without special dispensation), in which case there are ceremonies of Proclamation and also ceremonies of Induction where a Past Principal is going back in one of the Chairs.

It cannot be said with any degree of certainty when Principals of Royal Arch Chapters started to be installed in their chairs in ceremonies accompanied by the possession of specific secrets. Bernard E. Jones is of the opinion that in the early days of the Moderns' Grand Chapter it was more a matter of investment than installation.[66] This could possibly have been accompanied by a promise to act constitutionally and with impartiality.

Certainly with the revision of the ritual after the Royal Arch Union of 1817 and the key year of 1835 in the restructuring of the Royal Arch, we begin to see recognisable ceremonies of the Installation appearing.

Those Installation ceremonies have changed over the years. I have in my possession a ritual of the Complete Workings dated 1935 and it would seem that back then everyone below the rank of Principal was excluded from the conclaves in which the ceremonies were performed. They would bring in the Third Principal Elect, obligate him and then proceed to give

---

66 Bernard E. Jones – *Freemasons' Book of the Royal Arch*

him the secrets. He would then be asked to leave and they would do the same for the Second and then the First Principal. At the end of each Installation the newly installed Principal was saluted. These days, there are no salutes in the Royal Arch so we must assume it was either with the Grand or Royal Sign or with the sign peculiar to that Principal given once, twice or three times. We can probably assume the latter because no salutes are specified outside the conclaves for the Installation of Principals. I remember from one Chapter history I wrote that salutes were still being given in 1944.

It seems that gradually ordinary Companions have been allowed to see more and more of the Installation ceremonies so that now only the esoteric parts are conferred privately.

Central to each Installation ceremony is the scripture reading given, sometimes whilst all the Companions are present and sometimes just in the presence of Principals.

The readings are specially selected for the Installation of each Principal and are taken from various places in the Old Testament. Every ritual that I have come across uses the same readings which may well have been chosen by the Chief Rabbi to whom the Duke of Sussex went for advice. Some clarification of what is actually read may help. I have taken the liberty of using modern translations of the scriptures for ease of understanding. For expediency these readings are sometimes shortened but the full text is produced here.

Beginning with the Third Principal, Joshua, the readings are from Leviticus 8: 1-12, Numbers 16: 46-48 and Genesis 33:20 in that order. The Leviticus text relates the story of the ordination of Aaron and his sons:

The LORD said to Moses, 'Bring Aaron and his sons, their garments, the anointing oil, the bull for the sin offering, the two rams and the basket containing bread made without yeast, and gather the entire assembly at the entrance to the tent of meeting.' Moses did as the LORD commanded him, and the assembly gathered at the entrance to the tent of meeting.

This tent of meeting is the Tabernacle in the wilderness of Sinai erected by Moses, Aholiab and Bezaleel, known in Royal Arch Masonry as the 'First or Holy Lodge'.

Moses said to the assembly, 'This is what the LORD has commanded to be done.' Then Moses brought Aaron and his sons forward and washed them with water. He put the tunic on Aaron, tied the sash around him, clothed him with the robe and put the ephod on him. He also fastened the ephod with a decorative waistband, which he tied around him. He placed the breastpiece on him and put the Urim and Thummim in the breastpiece. Then he placed the turban on Aaron's head and set the gold plate, the sacred emblem, on the front of it, as the LORD commanded Moses.

Then Moses took the anointing oil and anointed the tabernacle and everything in it, and so consecrated them. He sprinkled some of the oil on the altar seven times, anointing the altar and all its utensils and the basin with its stand, to consecrate them. He poured some of the anointing oil on Aaron's head and anointed him to consecrate him.

For breastpiece, read breastplate, but there are two other terms that we need to look at. What was the ephod? And what has it got to do with a Royal Arch Companion becoming Third Principal of his Chapter? Bear in mind that the passage quoted is about ordination – becoming a priest. First he puts on a tunic, then a robe and then the ephod which is a sort of base or undergarment on which high priest's breastplate will rest. We have already looked at the stones in the breastplate, but what of the Urim and the Thummim? There is not much information about them in the Bible but we can possibly assume that they were probably gemstones and rather like a pair of dice, given that they were small enough to be placed IN the breastplate where they may have been contained in some sort of pouch. They were consulted on an oracular basis to determine God's will in various circumstances. Urim means 'lights' and Thummim means 'perfections' but whether they lit up or bore legends with words like 'true' and 'false', we know not. What is clear from the scripture is that they were clearly a symbol of authority and part of the regalia of a high priest.

The reading then continues from the Book of Numbers as follows:

Then Moses said to Aaron, 'Take your censer and put incense in it, along with burning coals from the altar, and hurry to the assembly to make atonement for them. Wrath has come out from the LORD; the plague has started.' So Aaron did as Moses said, and ran into the midst of the assembly. The plague had already started among the people, but Aaron offered the incense and made atonement for them. He stood between the living and the dead, and the plague stopped.

To understand this passage we need to become familiar with the account of the rebellion against Moses and Aaron by Korah, Dathan and Abiram which will be familiar to anyone who has received the Degree of Grand High Priest in the Order of the Allied Masonic Degrees. The Lord is exceedingly angry with the rebels and causes the ground to open and swallow them up. Those that are left are visited by the plague but Moses supplicates the Lord's mercy and Aaron took his censer to make atonement for the people. Some 14,700 died before the plague was stayed.

Finally there is the verse from Genesis: *And Jacob came to Shalem. And he established there an altar and called it — —— ——.*

So, in the first two passages we learn about the appointment of a high priest and the unchallengeable authority that goes with the office. The last quote refers to Jacob setting up his altar and gives us the word of the chair. It is worth noting that some Chapters still retain the practice of anointing the Third Principal and censing the Chapter.

For Haggai the readings are taken from 1 Samuel 3:1-21, Exodus 6:6 and 14:21-27, Genesis 17:1 and 35:11.

The boy Samuel ministered before the LORD under Eli. In those days the word of the LORD was rare; there were not many visions.

One night Eli, whose eyes were becoming so weak that he could barely see, was lying down in his usual place. The lamp of God had not yet gone out, and Samuel was lying down in the house of the LORD, where the ark of God was. Then the LORD called Samuel.

Samuel answered, 'Here I am.' And he ran to Eli and said, 'Here I am; you called me.'

But Eli said, 'I did not call; go back and lie down.' So he went and lay down.

Again the LORD called, 'Samuel!' And Samuel got up and went to Eli and said, 'Here I am; you called me.'

'My son,' Eli said, 'I did not call; go back and lie down.'

Now Samuel did not yet know the LORD: The word of the LORD had not yet been revealed to him.

A third time the LORD called, 'Samuel!' And Samuel got up and went to Eli and said, 'Here I am; you called me.'

Then Eli realised that the LORD was calling the boy. So Eli told Samuel, 'Go and lie down, and if he calls you, say, 'Speak, LORD, for your servant is listening.'' So Samuel went and lay down in his place.

The LORD came and stood there, calling as at the other times, 'Samuel! Samuel!'

Then Samuel said, 'Speak, for your servant is listening.'

And the LORD said to Samuel: 'See, I am about to do something in Israel that will make the ears of everyone who hears about it tingle. At that time I will carry out against Eli everything I spoke against his family—from beginning to end. For I told him that I would judge his family forever because of the sin he knew about; his sons blasphemed God, and he failed to restrain them. Therefore I swore to the house of Eli, 'The guilt of Eli's house will never be atoned for by sacrifice or offering.''

Samuel lay down until morning and then opened the doors of the house of the LORD. He was afraid to tell Eli the vision, but Eli called him and said, 'Samuel, my son.'

Samuel answered, 'Here I am.'

'What was it he said to you?' Eli asked. 'Do not hide it from me. May God deal with you, be it ever so severely, if you hide from me anything he told you.' So Samuel told him everything, hiding nothing from him. Then Eli said, 'He is the LORD; let him do what is good in his eyes.'

The LORD was with Samuel as he grew up, and he let none of Samuel's words fall to the ground. And all Israel from Dan to Beersheba recognized that Samuel was attested as a prophet of the LORD. The LORD continued to appear at Shiloh, and there he revealed himself to Samuel through his word.

Much as the reading of the previous chair is about the appointment and consecration of a high priest, so here we look at how Samuel was recognised as a prophet. Samuel, as a child, is the servant of Eli, and God calls him. The first verse tells us that God communicated through visions and what He said was obviously a great treasure, in the days before people could read the scriptures. Eli has fallen from grace, because of the blasphemy of his sons, which Eli failed to restrain, and his house is cursed. God tells Samuel this and Samuel informs Eli, who accepts the judgement of God. Then we are told that Samuel replaces Eli and is recognised throughout Israel as God's prophet.

Then we go back in time to Exodus 6:6 *Therefore, say to the Israelites: 'I am the LORD, and I will bring you out from under the yoke of the Egyptians. I will free you from being slaves to them, and I will redeem you with an outstretched arm and with mighty acts of judgment.'*

In this verse God commands Moses to instruct the people to follow him and God will lead them out of their Egyptian bondage.

Moses commanded the Israelites accordingly but, when push came to shove and Israelites saw the Egyptian army advancing on them, they were not too sure they had done the right thing:

As Pharaoh approached, the Israelites looked up, and there were the Egyptians, marching after them. They were terrified and cried out to the LORD. They said to Moses, 'Was it because there were no graves in Egypt that you brought us to the desert to die? What have you done to us by bringing us out of Egypt? Didn't we say to you in Egypt, 'Leave us alone; let us serve the Egyptians'? It would have been better for us to serve the Egyptians than to die in the desert!'

Moses answered the people, 'Do not be afraid. Stand firm and you will see the deliverance the LORD will bring you today. The Egyptians you see today you will never see again. The LORD will fight for you; you need only to be still.'

The story is continued in Exodus 14: 21-27:

Then Moses stretched out his hand over the sea, and all that night the LORD drove the sea back with a strong east wind and turned it into dry land. The waters were divided, and the Israelites went through the sea on dry ground, with a wall of water on their right and on their left.

The Egyptians pursued them, and all Pharaoh's horses and chariots and horsemen followed them into the sea. During the last watch of the night the LORD looked down from the pillar of fire and cloud at the Egyptian army and threw it into confusion. He jammed the wheels of their chariots so that they had difficulty driving. And the Egyptians said, 'Let's get away from the Israelites! The LORD is fighting for them against Egypt.'

Then the LORD said to Moses, 'Stretch out your hand over the sea so that the waters may flow back over the Egyptians and their chariots and horsemen.' Moses stretched out his hand over the sea, and at daybreak the sea went back to its place. The Egyptians were fleeing toward it, and the LORD swept them into the sea.

This well-known Bible story is fairly self-explanatory and also contains the first mention of the miraculous pillars of fire and cloud referred to in the Tracing Board Lecture of the Second Degree. It is worth noting that there is some debate amongst biblical scholars as to whether it was the Red Sea that was actually crossed. Further north, running from the River Jordan to Africa, is a marshy lake known as the Reed Sea (it is part of the Gulf of Aqaba which is known for its proliferation of reeds) and it is in this that the Egyptian chariots could have got bogged down.

John Mitchell confirms this opinion and also believes that the pillars of fire and cloud were stationary which is debatable because Exodus does say that the pillar of cloud moved in front of the Egyptians. He also queries the actual location of Mount Sinai (Mountain of the Moon) as the place where Moses received the Ten Commandments, as being not the (then) volcanic mountain on the Sinai peninsula but rather more likely to be Mount Bedr (Mountain of the Moon God) in modern day Saudi Arabia.[67]

The scripture reading concludes with two verses from the Book of Genesis, 17:1 and 35:11:

When Abram was ninety-nine years old, the LORD appeared to him and said, 'I am God Almighty; walk before me faithfully and be blameless.

And God said to him, 'I am God Almighty; be fruitful and increase in number. A nation and a community of nations will come from you, and kings will be among your descendants.

Both these verses say the same thing and the Hebrew translation of God Almighty gives us the word of the Second Chair.

Then finally for Zerubbabel they come from 1 Samuel 16:1-13, Exodus 3 vv 6 and 14, Exodus 6:3 and Psalm 68:4.

Not surprisingly, given that the previous two readings dealt with the callings of a high priest and a prophet, the reading to the First Principal elect is about the selection of a king:

The LORD said to Samuel, 'How long will you mourn for Saul, since I have rejected him as king over Israel? Fill your horn with oil and be on your way; I am sending you to Jesse of Bethlehem. I have chosen one of his sons to be king.'

But Samuel said, 'How can I go? If Saul hears about it, he will kill me.'

The LORD said, 'Take a heifer with you and say, 'I have come to sacrifice to the LORD.' Invite Jesse to the sacrifice, and I will show you what to do. You are to anoint for me the one I indicate.'

---

67 'Mount Sinai' by John Mitchell – *The Square* Magazine, March 2012

Samuel did what the LORD said. When he arrived at Bethlehem, the elders of the town trembled when they met him. They asked, 'Do you come in peace?'

Samuel replied, 'Yes, in peace; I have come to sacrifice to the LORD. Consecrate yourselves and come to the sacrifice with me.' Then he consecrated Jesse and his sons and invited them to the sacrifice.

When they arrived, Samuel saw Eliab and thought, 'Surely the LORD's anointed stands here before the LORD.'

But the LORD said to Samuel, 'Do not consider his appearance or his height, for I have rejected him. The LORD does not look at the things people look at. People look at the outward appearance, but the LORD looks at the heart.'

Then Jesse called Abinadab and had him pass in front of Samuel. But Samuel said, 'The LORD has not chosen this one either.' Jesse then had Shammah pass by, but Samuel said, 'Nor has the LORD chosen this one.' Jesse had seven of his sons pass before Samuel, but Samuel said to him, 'The LORD has not chosen these.' So he asked Jesse, 'Are these all the sons you have?'

'There is still the youngest,' Jesse answered. 'He is tending the sheep.'

Samuel said, 'Send for him; we will not sit down until he arrives.'

So he sent for him and had him brought in. He was glowing with health and had a fine appearance and handsome features.

Then the LORD said, 'Rise and anoint him; this is the one.'

So Samuel took the horn of oil and anointed him in the presence of his brothers, and from that day on the Spirit of the LORD came powerfully upon David. Samuel then went to Ramah.

So Samuel, prompted by the Lord, chooses David as the future King of Israel. Back again to Exodus:

Then he said, 'I am the God of your father, the God of Abraham, the God of Isaac and the God of Jacob.' At this, Moses hid his face, because he was afraid to look at God. God said to Moses, 'I AM WHO I AM. This is what you are to say to the Israelites: 'I AM has sent me to you'.

This is of course God speaking to Moses out of the burning bush, which we have already heard about in the Ceremony of Exaltation. Further on in chapter 6 of Exodus:

I appeared to Abraham, to Isaac and to Jacob as God Almighty, but by my name the LORD I did not make myself fully known to them.

So, from this we learn that the True Name of God was withheld from even the Patriarchs and was communicated for the first time to Moses.

Finally in Psalm 68 verse 4:

Sing to God, sing in praise of his name, extol him who rides on the clouds; rejoice before him – his name is JAH.

When each Principal has been read the scriptural extracts relevant to his chair, the Companions will retire and the Principals elect will again be presented by the DC to be installed (as we have seen, the order of that presentation varies with the ritual being used).

In the case of Joshua, the Third Principal, the ceremony of Ablution may be performed. The Installing Principal instructs him to take off his shoes and then, in a couple of rituals, pours water over his hands. The symbolism behind it is that he is removing his shoes as Moses did at the burning bush and washing his hands in allusion to the many 'washings and purifications' made before entering the priesthood, so that the new priest enters the service of God pure in body and mind.

In the Complete Working the new Principal repeats the words:

I will wash mine hands in innocency, thus will I compass Thine altar.

In Sussex ritual the Installing Principal says:

Wash you, make you clean; put away the evil of your doings from before your eyes; cease to do evil: learn to do well; seek judgement; relieve the oppressed.

Many Chapters now omit the ceremony of Ablution.

The Principal will then receive the signs and words of that chair and be invested with his robe and collar and entrusted with the sceptre of his office, pointing out the regal, prophetical and sacerdotal duties associated in each case, as discussed in Chapter 4. Where hats are worn they also bear devices of a regal, prophetical or sacerdotal nature.

In former times the next step after the Royal Arch was the degree of Knight Templar and those of us who know will remember that a KT Preceptory is opened in the Name of Christ, our Prophet, Christ our Priest and Christ our King.

When all three Principals have been installed, the ordinary Companions will re-enter the Chapter and in some rituals the Principals are proclaimed.

There then follow Robe Addresses given by the Immediate Past Z to the First Principal, the First Principal to the Second Principal and the Second Principal to the Third Principal. They sum up why the robes are the colour they are and also the peculiarities of the office in each case.

Offices will then be invested, for which there are short addresses in the rituals but this is often done just with suitable words.

In conclusion there are addresses to the Principals, Officers and Companions. These are too often overlooked which is a pity because they contain really beautiful language. The Address to the Principals (Complete Workings) includes the entrustment of the Charter, Royal Arch Regulations and Chapter by-laws.

CHAPTER 11

The Ceremony of the Passing of the Veils

We have already seen that the Veils ceremony is no longer worked in England, except in Chapters in Bristol where it was reintroduced in around 1910 as a revival of something that had previously existed.[68] It may also be noted that Bristol working in both Craft and Royal Arch has strong connections with Ireland, where of course the veils are still worked.

Veils in the Royal Arch Temple in Dublin.

In some places in the world the veils are part of the Royal Arch ceremony, whereas in others they constitute a separate degree, known variously as Excellent Mason, Excellent Master, Most Excellent Master and so forth. Increasing interest is being shown in the Veils ceremony among English Royal Arch Masons so it is pertinent to have a discussion of them here. Supreme Grand Chapter has now permitted one of the extant versions of the Veils ceremony to be demonstrated and several English Provincial Grand Chapters have done so or are planning to.

The colours of the veils are red or scarlet, blue, purple (which is of course an amalgam of red and blue) and white. In some jurisdictions the white veil was not used so that there were only three. These colours were those of the veils in the Temple and are also, of course, the colours of which our regalia and the border to some of our carpets are composed. The white veil seems to have been a later addition and its purpose will be made clear in a moment.

---

68 *Passing the Veils* by Sir Ernest Henry Cook AQC 85 1972

The Royal Arch ceremony that we know came to us in 1834 (although with some alteration since then as we have already seen), which was a year of major changes, as we have also seen. Officially the Ceremony of the Veils was dropped at this point, although there is evidence of Chapters continuing to work it as late as 1869 as an introductory part of the Royal Arch ceremony. That said, it is debatable whether Chapters under the Moderns' Grand Lodge before 1813 would have always worked it because their set-up was different. Under the Antients there was a 'career path' of the three Craft Degrees, then Mark Master, Passed Master (then a prerequisite for the Royal Arch), Excellent Mason (i.e. Veils), Royal Arch and Knight Templar. The Moderns did not officially have these additional degrees but the further you get away from London the more you find the Moderns adopting the practice of the Antients. This is especially true in Lancashire, where there was a particularly strong presence of Antients' lodges. For example the inventory of the Lodge of Peace and Unity No.314 (a Moderns' lodge in Preston) for 1817 lists 'Mark requisites'[69].

Some claim that the veils were done in a separate room from the Chapter proper but I have only ever seen them in the main temple. As those of you who are familiar with Rose Croix ceremonies will appreciate, it depends on the amount of accommodation available.

Bernard E. Jones in his *Freemasons' Book of the Royal Arch* writes;

The ceremony of passing the veils, which formed part of the Royal Arch ceremony in the late 18th Century, probably had a Christian origin, and was customary only during the period when the R.A. itself was largely a Christian degree. With the de-Christianization of the degree following, firstly, the union of the Grand Chapters in 1817 and, secondly, the drastic revision in 1835, the ceremony of the veils rapidly disappeared from English Royal Arch Masonry. [70]

The veils are, however, based on Old Testament events and are largely connected with Moses. There are different versions of the ceremony among those practised today but they do not vary too much.

Gilles Nullens says this: *The passing of the veils symbolises the enlightenment that comes with Masonic progression even if, originally, the veils were the emblems of the mysterious veil that was 'rent in twain' when the crucified Saviour passed through it. It could also have an alchemistic interpretation, or it is the symbol of the sufferings of the Jews in returning from exile.*

We appear, then, to have several different forms of symbolism in these

---

69 Bicentenary History of the Lodge of Peace and Unity No.314
70 *Freemasons' Book of the Royal Arch* by Bernard E. Jones

veils. Firstly we have things associated with Moses, recorded in the Book of Exodus. The things that happen at each veil happened to Moses as he wandered though the wilderness.

The colours of the veils were dictated by God. In Exodus chapter 26, we read:

Make the tabernacle with ten curtains of finely twisted linen and blue, purple and scarlet yarn, with cherubim woven into them by a skilled worker

This is again referred to in chapter 36.

But the ceremony itself is supposed to refer to obstacles encountered by returning Jews on their way to Jerusalem. That is whom the candidates (at one time there had to be three of them for the Royal Arch ceremony to be worked) are purporting to be. They get through these obstacles and then help with the rebuilding and make their discovery.

Then we have the Christian symbolism of the Veil of the Temple that was rent in twain after the crucifixion of Christ.

Finally there is the relationship of the colours of the veils with the four elements and hence with the Five Regular Platonic Bodies, the Royal Arch jewel and even the mysterious Triple Tau (although this had not come into use at the time the veils were being generally practised).

We don't know exactly when the ceremony was introduced but it is generally thought to be in the closing years of the eighteenth century. It could have come from Ireland because, I am informed, it has many similarities with the first degree of the Royal Black Institution (the 'higher degrees' of the Orange Order whose structure and ritual was based on Freemasonry). If that were the case it could have been introduced by the Antients' Grand Lodge, which again would make sense.

The Second Section of Richard Carlile's Royal Arch lectures/exposures, which first appeared in around 1825, and in which he admits the ceremony had been dispensed with in some Chapters, has this catechism:

Q. *How were you prepared to pass the veils?*

A. *I was blindfolded, both knees bare, both feet slip-shod and a cable tow round my waist.*

Q. *How did you gain admission to the first veil?*

A. *By four knocks, the Past Master's word and sign.*

Note that of course at that time and until 1835 one had to be a Past Master or Passed Master to even join the Royal Arch. After that time, the words Ammi Ruammah replaced the word of an Installed Master.

Q. Why were your feet slip-shod?

A. In allusion to the condition of Moses before the burning bush in the wilderness, who was told to put his shoes from off his feet, for the place whereon he stood was holy ground.

The baring of the feet continued in the ceremony of Ablution used in the Installation of a Third Principal.

Q. Why were you knees bare?

A. That I might offer up my prayers to the Great Jehovah, in the most humble manner, to thank him for mercies received, crave pardon for past offences and implore his aid and protection in my future conduct.

Q. Why was the cable-tow used?

A. In commemoration of a singular benefit derived from it by the Sojourners, in preparing the foundation of the second Temple.

Q. After entering the first veil, what happened to you?

A. I was led round and desired to be attentive to a portion of Scripture (Exodus 2:1–6) and when I halted the bandage was removed from my eyes.

Here we observe that the candidate was blindfolded for the Veils ceremony.

Q. What was then presented to your notice?

A. The Burning Bush. I was also entrusted with the pass words.

Q. Have you remembered those pass words?

A. I have.

Q. Will you give them to me?

A. – — ——— – —

Q. How did you pass the guard of the second veil?

A. By the benefit of the pass words I have just given.

Q. On entering the second veil what was presented to your notice and how were you disposed of?

A. The figure of a serpent and Aaron's rod were pointed out to me, and I was desired to be attentive to a portion of Scripture (Exodus 4:1–5) and was taught the sign and pass words.

Q. What is a sign?

A. Picking up Aaron's rod, in allusion to the serpent.

Q. Have you got the pass words?

A. I have.

Q. Will you give them to me?

A. ——, ——, ———.

Q. What gained you admission to the third veil?

The Ark of the
Covenant.

A.   The sign and pass words with which I was entrusted in the second veil.

Q.   On passing the third veil, what was said to you?

A.   I was again desired to be attentive to a portion of Scripture which was read to me
     (Exodus 4:6–9) and taught the signs and pass words to the sanctum sanctorum.

Q.   Can you give me those signs and pass words?

A.   I can (gives signs), ——————— — —— ——..

Q.   To what else was your attention directed in the third veil?

A.   I was shown the ark of the covenant, containing the tables of stone and the golden
     pot of manna, also the table of shew bread, the burning incense and the candlestick
     with seven branches.

Q.   Did those signs and pass words gain you admission to the sanctum sanctorum?

A.   They did.

Q.   How were you disposed of?

A.   I was desired to withdraw, to prepare for further instruction.

As you can see, this is a three-veil ceremony and when the candidate
comes back he receives the Royal Arch in the manner described in the
lectures in chapter 9. The passwords can vary from version to version. The
Royal Arch proper then followed.

The candidate(s) (remember there had to be three at one time) were
examined at each veil by the Captain of that veil. The names of these
officers vary from version to version but sometimes the first three veils are
staffed by the Principal Sojourner and the two Assistant Sojourners with
the last, White, Veil being in the charge of a Royal Arch Captain. Others

have a Principal then a Senior and Junior Sojourner and still others have officers called the Captains of the 1st, 2nd, 3rd and 4th Veils in which the Sojourners are conducting the candidate(s) through the ceremony. The end result is the same.

Various names are given in Veils ceremonies to the Three Master Masons from Babylon. In some versions they are called Shadrach, Meshach and Abednigo who, it may be remembered, were the three men consigned to the fiery furnace by Nebuchadnezzar when a fourth form appeared 'like unto the Son of God'. Despite the fact that the heat of the furnace was so great that Nebuchadnezzar's servants could not approach it, the three men inside remained unscathed. Another version names the three returning Master Masons as Joabert, Stolkin and either Adoniram or Guibelem. Both of these nomenclatures are fanciful: Shadrach and Co. would not have lived long enough to return to Israel and rebuild the Temple and a Joabert figures in the Scottish Rite Degree of Royal Arch of Enoch which is set centuries before. Further the three – Joabert, Stolkin and either Adoniram or Guibelem – were, according to another legend, supposed to have discovered a white pedestal with the name of God on top of it shortly after the death of Hiram Abif, again centuries before. But of course this is all legendary.

Neville Barker Cryer notes that, at Exmouth in Devon, there is still an Ark of the Covenant placed in front of the pedestal. He also notes that the Ark still appears on Supreme Grand Chapter certificates, which is no longer the case.[71]

But what of the fourth or white veil? This was meant to cover the place where the genuine secrets were held. Like the other veils there were signs and a pass word – the ones given in the third veil – and there are still vestiges of that final veil today. In most Chapters, the two Scribes unveil the pedestal when the candidate is first shown the word. In some Chapters, when the rest of the Companions go to tilt their banners the two Scribes stand at the eastern end of the Chapter. Now the two Scribes wear white surplices and the altar is covered by a white cloth. These are vestiges of the white veil. But what about the Sojourners? They wear white surplices as well. Normally the Second Sojourner is replaced by the candidate and goes and sits down. They wear white because they have passed through the white veil and visited the *sanctum sanctorum*.

The veils have been said to represent other things too. It has been claimed that they symbolise the four elements and the planets Saturn, Jupiter, Mars and Uranus in that order. The Jewish historian Josephus

---

71 Neville Barker Cryer – *What do you know about the Royal Arch?* – Lewis Masonic 2002

also claimed (he was talking about the Temple veils) that they had an astronomical significance in relation to the four elements. White signified earth because it was of white linen, made from flax ,a seed of the earth. Blue was the sky i.e. air. Red obviously meant fire and purple represented the sea because it was the colour of the Murex, a genus of sea snails. Whilst this last seems a little obscure the Murex were well known to the Ancients and are mentioned by Aristotle. White is, as in the Craft, an emblem of purity and innocence, blue of universal friendship, purple of unity and concord and red of zeal and fervency. If you read the Robe Addresses given to the Principals of a Royal Arch Chapter at their Installation it is easy to see from whence those addresses were derived.

There are versions of the Veils ceremony in which the candidate (at one time also there had to be three candidates for the ceremony to be performed) is attached by a rope which is drawn back so he then has to try again at the next veil.

Speaking personally, I would like to see the veils re-introduced into English Chapters. One can perceive Christian origins but I do not see how the ceremony could cause offence to anyone. The only thing it would do is to add interest. It has been said that what the Principal Sojourner does outside in our present ceremony is a form of substitute for the veils, but I cannot subscribe to that.

CHAPTER 12

How is the Royal Arch Practised in Other Parts of the World?

The Royal Arch originated in England although, as we have seen, it may have been based on something imported from France, where what existed early in the 18th century was probably contrived by people whose origins were in the British Isles.

The difference between England and the other Home Grand Lodges are chiefly that whereas in England the Royal Arch is an integral part of the Craft, in Scotland and Ireland it is independent (although obviously its members are also Craft Masons) and also that it is necessary in both these Constitutions to have a) received the Mark Degree and b) to have also received the Degree of Excellent Mason by passing the Veils. Many English Masons, being obliged to receive the Mark outwith their Craft Lodges or Royal Arch Chapters, have not done so and few outside Bristol will have passed the Veils. This makes a visit to a Chapter in Scotland or Ireland very difficult.

Bristol

OK so Bristol is not abroad. But their Royal Arch ceremony, partly because of their Irish connections, is sufficiently different to warrant our attention. We have already seen that the ceremony of Passing of the Veils was reintroduced into Bristol Chapters early in the 20th century. What is particularly interesting is what follows, but only for those who were exalted in Bristol Chapters. The Encampment of Baldwyn is a combination of the Knights Templar and Rose Croix Degrees and is described in the *Encyclopaedia of Freemasonry* thus:

There is at Bristol in England a famous Preceptory of Knights Templar, called the Baldwyn, which claims to have existed from time immemorial. This, together with the Chapter of Knights Rosae Crucis, is the continuation of the old Baldwyn Encampment, the name being derived from the Crusader, King of Jerusalem.

The earliest record preserved by this Preceptory is an authentic and important document dated December 20, 1780, and reads as follows:

'In the name of the Grand Architect of the Universe.

'The Supreme Grand and Royal Encampment of the Order of Knights Templars of St. John of Jerusalem, Knights Hospitallers and Knights of Malta, etc, etc.

'Whereas by Charter of Compact our Encampment is constituted the Supreme Grand and Royal Encampment of this Noble Order with full Power when Assembled

to issue, publish and make known to all our loving Knights Companions whatever may contribute to their knowledge not inconsistent with its general Laws. Also to constitute and appoint any Officer. or Officers to make and ordain such laws as from time to time may appear necessary to promote the Honor of our Noble Order in general and the more perfect government of our Supreme degree in particular.

We therefore the MOST EMINENT GRAND MASTER The Grand Master of the Order, the Grand Master Assistant General, and two Grand Standard Bearers and Knights Companions for that purpose in full Encampment Assembled do make known.'

Then follow twenty Statutes or Regulations for the government of the Order, and the document ends with 'Done at our Castle in Bristol 20th day of December 1780.'

It is not clear who were the parties to this 'Compact', but it is thought probable that it was the result of an agreement between the Bristol Encampment and another ancient body at Bath, the Camp of Antiquity, to establish a supreme direction of the Order. However that may be, it is clear that the Bristol Encampment was erected into a Supreme Grand Encampment in 1780. An early reference to the Knights Templar occurs in a Bristol newspaper of 25 January 1772, so it may fairly be assumed that the Baldwyn Preceptory had been in existence before the date of the Charter of Compact.

In 1791 the well-known Brother Thomas Dunckerley, who was Provincial Grand Master and Grand Superintendent of the Royal Arch Masons at Bristol, was requested by the Knights Templar of that city to be their Grand Master. He at once introduced great activity into the Order throughout England, and established the Grand Conclave in London – the forerunner of the Great Priory.

The seven Degrees of the Camp of Baldwyn at that time probably consisted of the three of the Craft and that of the Royal Arch, which were necessary qualifications of all candidates as set forth in the Charter of Compact, then that of the Knights Templar of St. John of Jerusalem, Palestine, Rhodes and Malta, that of the Knights Rose Croix of Heredom, the seventh being the Grand Elected Knights Kadosh.

About the year 1813 the three Degrees of Nine Elect, Kilwinning, and East, Sword and Eagle were adopted by the Encampment. The Kadosh having afterwards discontinued, the five Royal Orders of Masonic Knighthood, of which the Encampment consisted, were Nine Elect; Kilwinning; East, Sword and Eagle; Knight Templar; and the Rose Croix.

For many years the Grand Conclave in London was in abeyance, but when HRH the Duke of Sussex, who had been Grand Master since 1813, died in 1843, it was revived, and attempts were made to induce the Camp of Baldwyn to submit to its authority. These efforts were without avail, and in 1857 Baldwyn reasserted its position as a Supreme Grand and Royal Encampment, and shortly afterwards issued Charters to six subordinate Encampments. The chief cause of difference with the London Grand Conclave was the question of giving up the old custom of working the Rose Croix Degree within the Camp.

At last, in 1862, the Baldwyn was enrolled by virtue of a Charter of Compact 'under the Banner of the Grand Conclave of Masonic Knights Templar of England and Wales'. It was arranged that the Baldwyn Preceptory, as it was then called, should take precedence, with five others 'of time immemorial', of the other Preceptories; that it should be constituted a Provincial Grand Commandery or Priory of itself; and should be entitled to confer the degree of Knights of Malta.

In 1881 a Treaty of Union was made with the Supreme Council of the Thirty-third Degree, whereby the Baldwyn Rose Croix Chapter retained its time immemorial position and was placed at the head of the list of Chapters. It also became a District under the Supreme Council of the Thirty-third Degree and is therefore placed under an Inspector General of its own.

Scotland

The Supreme Grand Chapter of Scotland website says: 'The Royal Arch degree is not native to Scotland, but seems to have been introduced from both Irish and English sources, often Military Lodges, towards the middle of the 18th century. The first confirmed reference to a Royal Arch ceremony in a Scottish Lodge is contained within the Minutes of Lodge St. Andrew in Boston, Massachusetts, which is dated 1753.'

Military lodges introduced many other degrees beyond the Craft, and when the regiments moved on, lodges in the vicinity sometimes continued to work them. This situation continued until the end of the 18th century.

However, the early Secret Societies Acts caused the Grand Lodge of Scotland, in 1800, to issue a warning to its Lodges against the working of any degrees other than those of Entered Apprentice, Fellow Craft and Master Mason.

Scottish Royal Arch Jewel – obverse.

Many Lodges heeded the warning and the additional degrees associated with Royal Arch or Templar masonry had to be worked in assemblies separate from the lodge. The feeling grew amongst the Brethren that these assemblies should be legitimised in some way. A few obtained Charters from the Grand Encampment of Ireland. Others petitioned the Templar Grand Body in England and in 1810, under the patronage of the Duke

of Kent, the Royal Grand Conclave of Scotland was chartered and Alexander Deuchar appointed its first Grand Master.

This Royal Grand Conclave was empowered to grant Charters for the conferring of the Knight Templar grades upon those qualified as Royal Arch Masons. Deuchar soon realised that it was unsatisfactory to have the first three degrees and the Knight Templar grades under proper control but not the intermediate, qualifying, degrees of the Royal Arch.

In 1815 he convened a special committee, and all bodies in Scotland known to be working the Royal Arch degrees were contacted, with a view to forming a Grand Body to exercise proper control. All three Home Grand Lodges were consulted,

Scottish Royal Arch Jewel – reverse.

so as not to infringe upon their interests. Advice was sought, in particular, from England where the United Grand Lodge of England had recently been formed, and where the status of the Royal Arch degree had been acknowledged, as the completion of the Third Degree.

The Duke of Sussex was supportive, and advised Deuchar to make every effort to persuade the Grand Lodge of Scotland to adopt a similar stance, and take the Royal Arch under its wing. However, after an initially encouraging reply from the Grand Secretary of the Grand Lodge of Scotland, the matter became inextricably bogged down in committee.

The city of Edinburgh – home to the Supreme Grand Chapter of Scotland.

Eventually a meeting of interested Chapters could be delayed

no longer and, in August 1817, representatives of 34 Chapters met in Edinburgh and the Supreme Grand Chapter was erected and consecrated. Charters were issued, and the new Grand Body grew slowly but steadily, and gradually all bodies working the Royal Arch degree in Scotland came under its control.

At its peak, in the 1960s, the Supreme Grand Chapter of Scotland had some 650 active Chapters, many of which subsequently left to form Supreme Grand Royal Arch Chapters of their own, as happened for example in Israel and New South Wales.

There are, currently, some 470 active Chapters, 220 of which are overseas.

Royal Arch First Principal's Jewel (High Priest Zerubbabel)

Robert Cooper points out that both the Royal Arch and Knights Templar degrees were viewed with great suspicion as 'foreign' and not consistent with the Three Degrees of Craft Masonry as practised in Scotland. However, by dint of hard work and perseverance, a Grand Chapter was erected in 1817 as we see above and now functions completely separately from the Grand Lodge of the Craft.

There are certain differences between the English and Scottish working of the Royal Arch although they arrive at the same point in the end. The Officers of the Chapter are similar except that the Scots call their Sojourners the First, Second and Third Sojourners, instead of a Principal and two Assistants. They have the additional offices of Sword Bearer and Standard Bearer and also Captains of the Blue, Purple and Scarlet Veils.

The Mark Degree (which can be conferred either in a Craft Lodge or in a Royal Arch Chapter but usually the former) is an essential prerequisite as are the Veils. A Brother of the Craft does not have to be an Installed Master before proceeding to the Chapter Chairs, as is now also the case in England.

Scottish Chapters have a large arch supported by two columns which stands in between the pedestal and the Principals. The banners will be hung on the wall.

The stone which is removed to enter the vault is called a plug stone, rather than a keystone. It has seven sides and is the copestone, rather than a keystone.

Scottish Royal Arch Lectures are similar to the English but, in my view, rather more user-friendly.

Of the Holy Royal Arch of Jerusalem

Companions, the discovery which has been made is of the greatest importance, and you see that the world is indebted to Masonry for the preservation of the Book of the Sacred Law. Had it not been for the wisdom and precaution of our first Grand Master in constructing under the Temple a secret vault, which remained proof against the devouring flames, and fury of the enemy, this the only remaining copy of the Law, would have been lost at the destruction of the Temple. The characters on the triangle – the meaning of which the Sojourners could not understand – represent, as has been suggested to us by the, learned Sanhedrin, the name of God in three different languages; and all indicate, in our opinion, the true and long lost method of pronouncing the Sacred Word inscribed upon the circle; for it is of too essential a nature to be comprehended by human wisdom, or pronounced by the tongue of any individual. Lastly, Masonic tradition informs us, that the ancient Master Mason's word – lost at the building of King Solomon's Temple would one day be recovered and as the Jewel which the Sanhedrin discovered bears the mark of Hiram Abif there can be no doubt that the characters on the triangle signify that lost word and the manner of pronouncing it, for we know that it could only be imparted when the three Grand Masters were present, and consented to give it.

In future it shall be adopted as the Grand Word of the Royal Arch degree, and let it never be spoken unless in the manner I shall now proceed to explain. (This is done)

Our ordinary signs are five in number.

The First or P. S. which is given thus (it is demonstrated), and refers to the Soj. guarding his eyes from the intensity of the sun's rays, when their reflection shone so brilliantly on the gold plate found on the pedestal.

The Second is the sign of Salute, called also the Reverential is given so (it is demonstrated), and refers to the second ascent from the vault. Tradition informs us that the Sojourner, on bringing up the Roll from the vault, bound his two companions to secrecy by the P. s., he himself being obliged to use his left hand, as his right was occupied with the Roll.

The Third is the Penitential or Supplicatory s., given so (it is demonstrated), in allusion to the thankfulness of the chiefs of the Sanhedrin when they recovered the long lost Book of the Law.

The Fourth is the Monitorial or sign of Suffering, given so (it is demonstrated), in allusion to the descent of the Sojourner into the vault,

The Fifth, called the Fiducial sign is made thus, (it is demonstrated) in allusion to the Sojourner prostrating himself before the pedestal when he discovered what it was.

The Grand sign refers to the opening of the arches by the removal of the three stones, which stones are typified by the three Principals Z. H. and J. The three halts in giving it, and the three arches formed by the three Ps. allude to the three descents of the Sojourners before they discovered the mysterious triangle.

The Rods we use as emblems of power; as such they have been employed by all nations, but we use them in commemoration of the Rod wherewith Moses wrought so many wonders in the land of Egypt and in the wilderness. You have received explanations of the five ordinary signs deduced from the important discoveries made by the three Sojourners; but these signs may also have been adopted from other considerations.

The P. sign reminds us of the fall of Adam, and the dreadful penalty thereby entailed on his posterity, no less than death. We should therefore bow with resignation before the chastening hand of the living God, engrafting at the same time His law on our hearts; hence the R. s. In this expressive form the father of the human race presented himself before his offended Judge, and listened to the denunciation of his first and terrible judgment, and it was in after times adopted by Moses at the foot of Mount Horeb, where the Lord God appeared to him in the burning bush, to support the dazzling radiance of the Deity, he shielded his eyes from the divine splendour, at the time placing his hand on his heart in token of submission and obedience. The Penitential sign denotes state of heart and mind, without which our prayers and oblations can never be acceptable at the throne of grace, before which how should a frail and erring creature of the dust present himself, but with uplifted hands and bended knees betokening at once his humility and dependence. In this humble posture Adam first presented himself before God, and blessed the author of his being; again did he thus present himself before his offended Judge when he endeavoured to avert His wrath, and conciliate His mercy; and this expressive and contrite form he has handed down to posterity forever.

The M s. reminds us of the weakness of human nature, unable itself to resist the powers of darkness without that help which comes from above. By the action itself we acknowledge our own frailty and feebleness, and confess that we can do no good nor acceptable service but through strengthening power and mercy of the Most High without whose special favour we must ever be found unprofitable servants in His sight. Therefore, according to the manner adopted by our holy ancestors and like practised by the atoning Priests, we show by this, the F.s, the outward form of contrition and humility, as if would prostrate ourselves with our faces to the earth, and throw ourselves upon the mercies of the living God, looking forward with a becoming confidence to the accomplishment of His gracious promises by which alone we shall be enabled to pass through the ark of our redemption into those mansions of bliss and glory, and into the presence of Him who is the Great I Am, the Alpha and Omega, the First and the Last.

We should note that, in addition to the five signs used in England, there is also the Grand Sign. They are also claiming that the Sojourners made THREE descents into the vault.

Our Jewel is deserving of your attention.

On the bottom scroll is inscribed the motto 'Nil nisi clavis deest, nothing but the key is wanting', which may be taken in its literal sense. Then the Circle is an emblem of eternity with the motto 'Talia si jungere possis sit tibi scire satis, if thou comprehendest these things thou knowest enough.'

Within we have a chequered pavement to represent the uncertainty of life, and the instability of things terrestrial; and on it the representation of a pedestal of pure white marble, in the form of the altar of incense, being the true double cube, and, therefore, both in figure and colour the perfect emblem of innocence and purity.

The whole delineates the secret vault with the rays of the meridian sun illuminating the Altar, the Book of the Holy Law being placed thereon. Instead of the representation of the vault, we sometimes find on Royal Arch jewels, within the circle, two intersecting triangles said to denote the elements of fire and water, and with the motto 'Deo regi fratribus honor fidelitas benevolentia,' thus declaring that the wearer is desirous of doing his duty, and of filling up with justice that link in the chain of creation wherein his Great Creator hath thought proper to place him. Within this is another triangle with the sun in its centre, its rays issuing forth at every point – an emblem of the Deity – represented by a circle whose centre is everywhere and circumference nowhere, denoting His omnipresence and perfection; it in also an emblem of Geometry; and here also we find the perfect emblem of the science of Agriculture pointed out by a pair of compasses issuing from the centre of the sun, and suspending a globe, denoting the earth, and thereby indicating the influence of that glorious luminary over both animal and vegetable creation; admonishing us to be careful to perform every operation in its proper season, that we lose not the fruits of our labour.

Underneath these is the compound character known as the Triple Tau one of the Royal Arch mason's emblems. This mystical character signifies in its figurative appearance Hiram of Tyre, or Hiram Abif the letters bearing the same Phoenician import as they do with us. It signifies also T. H., Templum Hierosolyma the Temple of Jerusalem, and is used as the Royal Arch symbol, whereby the wearer acknowledges himself a servant of the true God; who had there established His worship, and to whose service that glorious Temple was erected. The Royal Arch symbol therefore may aptly recall to our minds our constant duty to offer worship to The Great Elohim; The Most High: The Everlasting: The Almighty God.

The equilateral triangle was much revered by ancient nations as containing the greatest and most abstruse mysteries, and as a symbol of God, denoting a Triad of Intelligence, a Triad of Deity, a Triune God. Moreover, the Tetragrammaton, or incommunicable name was written by the Jews in a triangular form: the initial letter denoting the thought, the idea of God, a ray of light too transcendent to be contemplated by mortal eye; this name of God, the Tetragrammaton, could not be more aptly placed than in the symbol, or triangle, itself and hence the true meaning of the Royal Arch double triangle, but originally represented thus. So that while this sacred emblem was deservedly revered by the Jews, both it and the double triangle itself are adopted as Royal Arch symbols.

In a Royal Arch Chapter we have seven lights placed in the angles and centre of our double triangle. Some interpret the three greater and the three lesser as if identical with those explained to you in the Entered Apprentice degree, while others consider them symbolical of wisdom, strength, and beauty; and truth, concord, and peace, well known expressions illustrative of our Order, but the more learned Jews consider the three greater lights to represent Wisdom, Truth, and Justice, while Christians consider them as emblematical of the Trinity. The three lesser will then exhibit the three Principals, and also the moral and religious light which is derived from the Patriarchal, Mosaical, and Prophetical dispensations. The whole taken together being emblematical of the beauty and harmony which is visible in all the works of Nature, where nothing is wanting nor anything superfluous. By all the central beam from the Altar is held to be that which irradiates the whole. The seven lights may also be held to represent externally the ordinary three great lights of masonry, while the inner four show forth the Tetragrammaton itself.

In approaching the Altar you were commanded to halt seven times and make obeisance at the third, fifth, and seventh step. The same practice is said to have been observed by the Most Excellent Grand Master, King Solomon, on passing each of the seven pillars which supported the arch of the private gallery through which he passed daily to offer up his praises to the Almighty. It ought to remind you of the works of Creation, to keep the seventh day holy also of the seven months required, for the erection of the Tabernacle as likewise of the seven complete years for the building of the Temple, and the seven additional months, six being added to finish the work, and the seventh in sacrifices and thanksgiving at the dedication.

This last paragraph is highly significant. As we saw previously the seven steps taken in the English Royal Arch are said to recall the Passing of the Veils and yet the Scots, who have passed the veils still take seven steps. This leads me to think that the seven steps taken by the candidate at his Exaltation recall the veils but the advance up the Chapter by the Principals at the opening is doing the same thing as in Scotland, i.e. halting and bowing in line with the practice of King Solomon. The further symbolism of the number seven is also interesting, as is the fact that the Scots have seven lights, whereas the English have only six.

LECTURE III
The Sacred Pedestal.

I shall now describe to you the Sacred Pedestal. A cube has ever been considered the symbol of equality, purity, and justice; so, therefore, the double cube was selected by our forefathers as the shape of the Altar of incense, being a type – in a superlative degree – of the purity, excellence, and durability of the divine power.

The characters on the front of the pedestal are the initials of the names and designations of the Grand Masters, who presided over the Sacred Lodge. They are delineated in Hebrew characters, thus:

Shelomoh Meleck Israel,

Huram, Meleck Tsur,

Huram. Ben Almanah,

Meaning Solomon King of Israel, Hiram King of Tyre, and Hiram the Widow's Son: or, Solomon Rex Israelis, Hiram Rex Tyri, Hiram Vidua Filius.

Below these characters near the foot of the pedestal is the Triple Tau.

Around the top of the pedestal are sculptured ornaments; the top itself should be of pure gold and illuminated from above, but we use enamelled glass illumined from below on it is a circle, and a triangle.

The Circle is an emblem of eternity having neither beginning nor end, and fitly reminds us of the purity, wisdom, and glory of the Omnipotent, which is without beginning or end.

The Triangle is a symbol of divine union, and an emblem of the mysterious Triune, equally representing the attributes of Deity, and His Triune essence. On the circle of gold you behold the great and awful name of God, the sacred, mysterious, and ineffable Tetragrammaton.

It is not in the power of any mortal adequately to solve or analyze the import or comprehensiveness of this word. Suffice it to observe that it implies the self-sufficient power of the Omnipotent, typifying the eternal duration of the Godhead, of that Great Being who is of, by, and from Himself, the origin and source of all power and majesty incomprehensible and that it denotes, with wonderful and peculiar accuracy, the eternally unchanged and unchangeable existence of the Almighty, who was, and is, and ever shall be the same great and living God. This awful name was held in such veneration by the children of Israel, that it was never uttered but once a year, and then only by the High Priest, when at a solemn assembly he entered the Sanctum Sanctorum or Holy of Holies, and after many religious ceremonies in propitiation of the nation's sins; and, at the present day, no true Israelite would dare to pronounce, or even write it, in his prayers, public or private, but invariably adopts the substitute words Adonai or El Shaddai. This word also implies that the God of Israel will be faithful to His promise, and keep the covenant He made with the seed of Abraham.

It is lawful for three Jews who are Royal Arch Masons to pronounce this Holy Word by the three distinct aspirations, but in no other way, and it is always pronounced by us in the same manner.

On the three sides of the triangle you behold the three sacred syllables, which collectively constitute the peculiar and grand word which you have sworn never to pronounce but in the presence of two or more Companions of this exalted order, and in the manner pointed out to you.

Of this mysterious compound the first syllable is a Chaldaic word signifying 'I Am.' It is also a Hebrew word which signifies 'I shall be' thus wonderfully referring to the present, future, and eternal existence of God. It also denotes the incomprehensible majesty of the Omnipotent, and is composed of two of the four letters of the Tetragrammaton. The second is a Syriac word, and signifies 'Lord' or 'Powerful'; but is also a compound word, being formed of a preposition, Beth, which in many oriental languages signifies 'In' or 'On,' and another expression, which implies 'Heaven' or 'On High.' The third, which is an Egyptian word, signifies 'Father of all'; it is also a Hebrew word implying 'Power.' The three syllables therefore, or the whole expression, convey the following divine import 'I am and shall be Lord in Heaven on High, the Powerful, the Father of all.'

Such is the account of the Pedestal, of the circle, and of the single triangle found by the Sojourners and from this we may infer that the equilateral triangle was the original mark or signature of a Master Mason, and the same as that preserved by the Mark Masters, which was pointed out to you in that degree. But the three ancient Principals of the Sanhedrin Zerubbabel, Haggai and Joshua added another triangle intersecting the former, on the sides of which they caused to be engraved the secret word of these offices. These cannot be imparted to you at present, as they are only given to Principals of Chapters.

The various significations of the double triangle itself have been described to you in the 2nd. lecture.

These lectures do not correspond exactly to the English ones – Historical, Symbolical and Mystical – but tend to finish up covering the same ground.

Ireland

Irish Royal Arch Masonry flourishes under the Supreme Grand Chapter of Ireland with Chapters organised into Districts throughout the island of Ireland and many Chapters abroad either in Districts, under Grand Superintendents, or operating directly under the Supreme Grand Chapter in Dublin. There is a Royal Arch Chapter of Research which is based in Dublin but travels throughout Ireland to hold its convocations.

The Irish Royal Arch Breast Jewel.

Irish Masonry is very ancient. Indeed there are references to it as far back as 1688 from records in Trinity College, Dublin.

The Masonic scene on the island of Ireland has been greatly affected by political and social developments. Religion also played a part, particularly after the American and French revolutions.

Ex. Comp. James Penny P.K. (Past King – see Appendix 3 for list of Irish Officers) sums this up very well as follows:

> Both the American and French revolutions sought to separate church and state. This did not go down well with the Papacy and three Papal Bulls were issued between 1738 and 1821, more or less branding the [Masonic] Order as the 'Devil incarnate'.

This gave rise to the cruel and unfair fiction that Freemasonry is anti-Catholic, which it is not and never has been. Nonetheless, Irish Catholics at the time paid little heed to these Bulls and continued to become Masons.

Another Bull, however, issued by Pope Leo XII was more successful and succeeded in halving the number of Masonic lodges in Ireland. Following the rising of the United Irishmen in 1798 when Catholic and Protestant fought together, after this Bull they became polarised and Freemasonry became associated with what James Penny calls the English and Protestant ascendancy. Following closely after that, Ireland had other things to occupy her attention with the potato famine of 1845–48, which was the beginning of the Irish diaspora. Add to that the 19th century Home Rule crisis, the struggle for independence followed by a civil war in the 1920s and the more recent troubles in the north of the country and it becomes a real tribute to the ability of Freemasonry to transcend the follies of mankind and to continue to practise brotherly love, relief and truth.

There are differences in the way the Irish work, chief among which is the enforcement of a uniform ritual in every Masonic order. As Robert Bashford says:

> Ritual is controlled by bodies known as The Grand Lodge / Grand Chapter of Instruction which have overall control of the ritual within their own particular rite. These Instructional bodies comprise of Elected Members from Brethren skilled in Ritual throughout the Irish Constitution and nominated representatives from both Grand Lodge & Provincial Grand Lodges, whose duty was to keep these bodies appraised of all current decisions and ruling in respect of ritual. Irish Workings for some three hundred years were a completely oral tradition with no official printed ritual.
>
> It has only been in the last few years that this tradition changed and Grand Lodge, with the approval of The Grand Lodge of Instruction, finally issued printed Ritual workings. In this way, up until modern time Irish ritual has been kept vibrant and alive, by the constant process of checks and balances imposed by the Grand Lodge of Instruction. Indeed the pinnacle of many Masonic careers, after years of Ritual work including participation in Degree Exemplifications in front of the Grand Lodge of Instruction is the invitation to become an Elected Member of this body, entitled to participate in both open and closed session.[72]

---

72 Robert T. Bashford – *The Gift of Irish Freemasonry*

This was the brainchild of one John Fowler who had a profound effect on Irish Masonry in general. Fowler, who had already served as Deputy Grand Master of Ireland between 1818 and 1824, and was to become Deputy Grand Secretary in 1834 from then until his death in 1856, was a veritable dictator on all matters of ritual. It was he who in 1814 took the initial steps towards safeguarding that ritual with the establishment of a Grand Lodge of Instruction on 10 January of that year at a meeting held at his own home, No.106 Mecklenburgh Street, Dublin. He also single-handedly removed a whole group of additional degrees which then existed in Ireland called Ark Mason, Mark Fellow Mason, Mark Mason, Link Mason or Wrestle, Babylonian Pass (or the Red Cross of Daniel), Jordan Pass, and Royal Order (or Prussian Blue).[73] None of these seem to have any connection with degrees we in England are now familiar with.

So we can see from this that the term Lodge or Chapter of Instruction has a very different meaning from what we in England understand it to be.

The first surprise we get when looking at Irish Royal Arch Masonry is in finding out that there are two Royal Arch Legends: firstly the one about the rebuilding of the Temple under Zerubbabel, which we in England are familiar with, and secondly the one currently used in Ireland which is about the repair of the Temple under King Josiah, in about 855 BC.

The story of Josiah is covered in 2 Chronicles 34 verses 1, 2, 8 and 14:

Josiah was eight years old when he became king, and he reigned in Jerusalem thirty-one years. He did what was right in the eyes of the LORD and followed the ways of his father David, not turning aside to the right or to the left.

In the eighteenth year of Josiah's reign, to purify the land and the temple, he sent Shaphan son of Azaliah and Maaseiah the ruler of the city, with Joah son of Joahaz, the recorder, to repair the temple of the LORD his God.

While they were bringing out the money that had been taken into the temple of the LORD, Hilkiah the priest found the Book of the Law of the LORD that had been given through Moses.

Royal Arch Masonry in Ireland enjoys a similar status to its English counterpart in that it is considered a part of Craft Freemasonry and of the Third Degree since 1814. However this is a little misleading because the Irish Grand Chapter is nonetheless independent of its Grand Lodge.[74]

In the 18th century, the structure of Irish Degrees was as follows:

First Degree: what we would now call Entered Apprentice and Fellowcraft combined.

---

73 Paper by Bro James Penny, Irish Lodge of Research
74 *Royal Arch Masonry in Ireland in the early 19th Century* by Bro R..W. Harvey, Transactions of the Irish Lodge of Research Vol 16 (1969–1975)

Second Degree: Master Mason based on the Hiramic legend.
Third Degree: Part 1. Royal Arch based on the Josiah legend.
Third Degree: Part 2. Royal Arch based on the Zerubbabel legend, which later became known as the Super Excellent. This evolved into what is now called Irish Knight Masonry, at first under the control of the Knights Templar and since 1923 under the Grand Council of Knight Masons.

This had changed by the early 19th century to three Craft Degrees followed by:

Fourth Degree: Past Master, as in England at that time.
Fifth Degree: Excellent Master (Veils).
Sixth Degree: Super Excellent Master.
Seventh Degree: Royal Arch.[75]

The position was a little less clear than this, however, and there were variations but, as has been pointed out in Harvey's article, the Grand Lodge of Ireland made little attempt to control matters and each lodge became a law unto itself. By the turn of that century it was becoming obvious that this would not do and, in 1805, a Grand Chapter was established to regulate matters.

We have seen in chapter 2 how the first mention of the Royal Arch anywhere was in Youghall, Co. Cork, in 1743. There is a further reference recorded in Faulkner's *Dublin Journal* 10-14 July 1754 under the heading 'St John's Day celebration by the Lodge in Youghall No21':

Imprimis, Sword drawn. The first Salutation on the Quay of Youghall, upon their coming out of their Lodge Chamber, was the Ships firing their guns with their colours flying,
Secondly, The first was a Concert (band) of music with two Sentinels with their Swords drawn,
Thirdly, Two Apprentices, bare headed, one with a twenty four Inch gauge, the other a common Gavel,
Fourthly, The Royal Arch carried by two excellent Masons Etc.

In spite of many vicissitudes there is still a Royal Arch Chapter in Youghall today. Because of trading links there have always been strong

---

75 *Royal Arch Masonry in Ireland in the early 19th Century* by Bro R..W. Harvey, Transactions of the Irish Lodge of Research Vol 16 (1969–1975)

connections with Masonry in County Cork (and particularly in Cork City, Kinsale and Youghall) and that practised in Bristol.

In Ireland one must be a Master Mason for at least twelve months before attaining the Royal Arch. There was formerly a Passed Master Degree, as in England (which it is claimed was introduced into England by Laurence Dermott, Grand Secretary of the Antients, but the requirement to have passed the chair was dropped in Ireland in 1864). The modern ceremony is preceded by the Mark Degree (although only since 1874) worked on a separate night from the Royal Arch, for which purpose the Chapter turns itself into a Mark Lodge with all the officers occupying corresponding positions (see Appendix 3). The Irish Mark ceremony is similar to the English and Scottish. The Veils ceremony comes next and finally the Royal Arch, based on the Josiah legend.

The Mark Room, Molesworth Street, Dublin. Photo courtesy of the Supreme Grand Chapter of Ireland.

An Irish Chapter room would probably appear very sparse compared to England: the banners are arranged at the side in front of the walls and there is a central altar with the VSL on. Each Principal has a small table or pedestal with RA emblems on it. The Companions wear their aprons under their jackets which some say is because they are going to take their coats off and do a bit of work!

Early in the 20th century a resolution was put before the Supreme Grand Chapter of Ireland to replace the Josiah legend with the Zerubbabel one so as to bring Ireland into line with other constitutions. It was summarily rejected. I will say it again – Masons don't like change!

James Penny gives a useful description of the modern Irish Royal Arch ceremony:

The room will be divided by four coloured veils, blue, purple, scarlet and white, which are hung North South, and divide the room East to West. The colours not only parallel those of the Tabernacle the tent like structure that housed the Ark of the Covenant during the Children of Israel wandering in the wilderness but also the four ancient elements, air, water, fire and earth. All are guarded by Captains except the Captain of the White veil who is however known as the Royal Arch Captain. All have small Banners similar to the colours of their respective veils; on these banners is a six pointed star in the centre of which is a Triple Tau. n.b. these are the only banners in an Irish Chapter. The white

The Royal Arch Room, Dublin (note the veils). Photo courtesy of the Supreme Grand Chapter of Ireland.

The Royal Arch Room, Dublin (note the position of the banners. Photo courtesy of the Supreme Grand Chapter of Ireland.

veil separates the Council Chamber from the rest of the room; the Superintendent of the Tabernacle sits inside the Council Chamber within the White veil and the Captain of the Host sits in front of the three principal Officers, named as the Chief Scribe, High Priest and the Excellent King; these represent Shaphan, Hilkiah and Josiah although they are never named in the ceremony. The altar is in its traditional place in the centre of the Lodge Room and will have a special compartment let into the top; this will have a lid with a ring fitted to enable the crow bar to be inserted. Some Halls have a proper vault in the floor; unfortunately due to health and safety considerations they are rarely used to-day as they were intended. However, there is always a light to illuminate the magnificent plate of gold!

The ritual may appear simple to Scottish and English Companions, but it is worth giving a brief outline: before the chapter is opened the Ex. King will instruct any who are not Royal Arch Masons to retire; this is obviously retained from the time all degrees were worked under the Craft Warrants. After proving the Chapter tyled and guarded next the Captain of the Host is asked if he can vouch all present as Royal Arch Masons (No password is given); when the Captain of the Host gives this assurance the Officers of the Chapter are asked to take their places. The Captain is next instructed to announce to the Companions to divide the word; all divide the word.

In Ireland the word is the old tripartite one despite a move to change to the one now used in England and Scotland; a ground swell of opinion from the Irish Companions stopped this change. The Captain of the Host will have to assure the Ex. King that the symbols used in our ceremonies are safely preserved and duly deposited. After a prayer, during which the banners are lowered, the Chapter is declared open.

The degree is divided into two parts, Reception and passing the Veils and the Degree of the Royal Arch. The Candidate(s) are hoodwinked on entry into the chapter room, (it is preferable to have three candidates but a Companion can make up the number); they then pass under an arch made with the hands of the Brethren, then they take an obligation as a Royal Arch Mason after which they are conducted to the Blue veil where they are challenged by its Captain for the password; this being given by his conductor they are now admitted and instructed in the password and sign for passing the veil. This ceremony is repeated for the purple and red veils. The candidates are now admitted into the Council Chamber where they express their desire to help with the work of repairing the Temple; the candidates having received permission to assist with the work leave the room. They return in the attire of workmen i.e. they are in their shirt sleeves and commence to clear the rubble with a spade, and discover the secret vault when the pick strikes its top to produce a hollow sound, and lift the ring in the top with the crow bar; if there is one candidate he will be figuratively lowered into the vault to discover the items left there by our three Grand Masters which will be explained to him by his conductor. Brethren this is a much truncated version of the degree; there are no ceremonies at the festive board as in England.

It is common to hear the Chapter referred to as the red, as the regalia as worn in the Chapter is all red and consists of an apron and sash worn from right shoulder to left hip, and in certain Chapters white gloves. As in the two other Home constitutions a member Jewel on a white ribbon may be worn but it is more usual to see the Past King's one on a red ribbon and since 1991 a past V. W. Master's jewel [from the Mark Degree] is also permitted in Chapter but it is not permitted to wear Chapter jewels in Craft Lodges although most people would be too polite to pass comment on a visitor doing so. The inscriptions on a Royal Arch jewel are as follows, round the circle 'SIT TIBI SCIRE SATIS SI TALIA JUNGERE POSSI' (If you canst unite such things thou knowest enough). On five sides of the two triangles are inscribed in Greek, Latin and English (O, worshipper of God citizen of the world).[76]

---

76 James Penny – Paper in Irish Lodge of Research

Continental Europe and North America

In much of the European continent as also in the USA and Canada (but see Appendix 2), the Royal Arch is conferred as part of what is called the York Rite.

Once a Mason has received the Craft Degrees or what Americans call the Degrees of the Blue Lodge, two main paths are open to him: The Scottish Rite (see Appendix 2 for a list of the degrees) which is by no means unconnected with the Royal Arch and the York Rite which includes the Royal Arch. We shall concern ourselves with the latter.

The sequence of degrees in the York Rite may vary slightly between jurisdictions (see Appendix 1) but, in Greece, it is as follows:

Craft Degrees
Mark Master
Passed Master
Excellent Master
Royal Arch (including the Veils)
Cryptic Degrees
Red Cross
Knight of Malta
Knight Templar

Despite the fact that some claim the Degree came originally from France, the Royal Arch has never been very strong there. There is a *Grande Chapitre pour l'Arch Royale de la France* and that controls it but, due to the variation in French Craft rituals' interest is perhaps more limited than elsewhere. The French-speaking Canadian Province of Quebec also has a *Grande Chapitre*.

Much of the rest of the world originated from England, Scotland and Ireland and practises the Degree in the manner of the Mother country. In time these areas formed their own Grand Chapters and went their own way.

To give an idea of how regalia varies in different constitutions, below is a picture by courtesy of the Supreme Grand Chapter of British Columbia and the Yukon, taken when they were presenting a cheque to Eagle Ridge Hospital Foundation, Port Moody:

Appendices

The York Rite: Sequence of Degrees

Throughout North America and also in Europe the Royal Arch Degree is worked as part of the York Rite. In Canada that rite is subdivided into three sections as follows:

Symbolic or Craft Masonry
1. Entered Apprentice
2. Fellowcraft
3. Master Mason

Capitular Masonry
4. Mark Master Mason
5. Virtual Past Master
6. Most Excellent Master (the Passing of the Veils)
7. Royal Arch

Cryptic Masonry
8. Royal Master.
9. Select Master.
10. Super Excellent Master.
11. Red Cross of Babylon.

Jurisdictions in the United States add some more degrees to this list:

Chivalric Masonry
1. Illustrious Order of the Red Cross
2. Order of Malta (including the Pass Degree of Mediterranean Pass or Knight of St.Paul)
3. Order of the Temple

Much of this will seem strange to English eyes but, believe it or not, all of these degrees, with the exception of Virtual Past (or Passed) Master are available in England and Wales. Looking at the Capitular Masonry group, we have already seen that the Mark Degree is not a prerequisite for Capitular (or Chapter) Masonry in England as it is in most jurisdictions. The Virtual Past Master was a device to enable people to 'Pass' the Chair so as to qualify them to join the Royal Arch, which was necessary up to 1834. They would be given the secrets of an Installed Master without actually having been in the Chair of a lodge. It has been said that the ritual resembled the Extended Working of the Board of Installed Masters, which most English Masons have never seen, but which is practised in Royal Cumberland Lodge No.41 in Bath and in various places in the north of England. However, having seen the ritual for the degree as now worked in Iowa and Indiana, I can discern very little connection.

The Most Excellent Master referred to above is the Passing of the Veils. A degree of that name exists in the Cryptic Rite in England which we will look at in a moment, but it is not the Veils and is completely different.

Moving on to the Cryptic group, or what is more properly called in England the Order of Royal and Select Masters, the first three degrees listed are part of the English Cryptic, together with the Most Excellent Master which, as we have seen, is different from its American namesake. The order of conferment is Select Master, Royal Master, Most Excellent Master and Super Excellent Master. The best way to describe the Cryptic rite is that whereas the Craft is about the building of the First Temple and the Royal Arch is about the building of the Second, the Cryptic is about what happened in between. It is nonetheless necessary to be both a Mark Mason and a Royal Arch Mason to join the Cryptic in England.

The Red Cross of Babylon Degree is one of the degrees of the Order of the Allied Masonic Degrees in England. It has strong similarities with the rituals of Knight Masonry as practised in Ireland and the US, as well as with the 15th Degree of Knight of the Sword or of the East in the Ancient and Accepted Scottish Rite or Rose Croix.

APPENDIX 2
The Ancient and Accepted Scottish Rite: Sequence of Degrees

Having described the York Rite it seems sensible to talk now about the Scottish Rite as worked in North America and Europe (but not in Scotland) because some of its degrees bear a distinct relationship to the Royal Arch

The degree structure of the The Ancient and Accepted Scottish Rite is comprised as follows:

Craft Degrees

1. Entered Apprenctice
2. Fellow Craft
3. Master Mason
Intermediate Degrees

4. Secret Master

5. Perfect Master

6. Intimate Secretary

7. Provost and Judge

8. Intendant of the Buildings

9. Elect of Nine

10. Elect of Fifteen

11. Sublime Elect

12. Grand Master Architect

Referring to the Legend of the Secret Vault and its contents)

13. Royal Arch of Enoch (Sometimes called Knights of the Ninth Arch or Royal Arch of Solomon)*

14. Grand, Elect, Perfect and Sublime Master*

Historical Degrees or Orders of Chivalry

15. Knight of the Sword or Of the East*

16. Prince of Jerusalem *

First of the Philosophical Degrees

17. Knights of the East and West

The Rose Croix Proper

18. Knight of the Rose Croix

Areopagus Degrees

19. Grand Pontiff

20. Grand Master of all Symbolic Losdges or Master Ad Vitam

21. Noachite, A Prussian Knight *

22. Knight of the Royal Axe, or Prince of Libanus

23. Chief of the Tabernacle

24. Prince of the Tabernacle

25. Knight of the Brazen Serpent

26. Prince of Mercy, or Scottish Trinitarian

27. Grand Commander of the Temple

28. Knight of the Sun

29. Knight of St Andrew, or Patriarch of the Crusades

The remaining degrees are individual and are conferred on merit.

30. Grand Elect Knight Kadosh, also styled Knight of the Black and White Eagle

31. Grand Inspector, Inquisitor, Commander
32. Sublime Prince of the Royal Secret
33. Sovereign Grand Inspector General

In some countries the 4th, 9th, 14th, 18th, 30th, 31st and 32nd are conferred 'in extenso' and the rest are conferred by name. The rite today is what remains of probably about 800 degrees which were around in the 18th and 19th centuries The degrees which are not given in extenso are communicated by name. In England, the 18th, 30th, 31st and 32nd are the only ones given in extenso, although demonstrations of the Intermediate Degrees are given annually. Those degrees marked with * have a content which is closely akin to the Passing of the Veils and the Royal Arch.

APPENDIX 3

The Officers of an Irish Royal Arch Chapter

(It should be noted that the Mark Degree is taken within RA Chapters in Ireland and the Chapter turns itself into a Mark Lodge for that purpose, hence the corresponding Mark ranks shown)

Chapter Office	Mark Office
Excellent King	V.W.M.
High Priest	S.W.
Chief Scribe	J.W.
Treasurer	
Registrar	Sec
Director of Ceremonies	
Almoner	
Chaplain	Chaplain
Captain of the Host	M.O.
Superintendent of the Tabernacle	
Royal Arch Captain	S.O.
Captain of the Scarlet Veil	J.O.
Captain of the Purple Veil	S.D.
Captain of the Blue Veil	J.D.
Janitor	I.G.
Stewards	

APPENDIX 4

The Officers of a Scottish Royal Arch Chapter

First Principal/Zerubbabel
Second Principal/Haggai
Third Principal/Jeshua
Scribe Ezra
Scribe Nehemiah
Treasurer
First Sojourner
Second Sojourner
Third Sojourner
Sword Bearer
Director of Ceremonies
Superintendent of Works
Standard Bearer
Captain of the Blue Veil
Captain of the Purple Veil
Captain of the Scarlet Veil
Organist
Steward
Janitor

APPENDIX 5

Othello Chapter No.5670, Larnaca, Cyprus
Catechetical Explanation of the Exaltation Ceremony
Part One

Introduction

Companions, the catechism which follows is intended to explain aspects of the Ceremony of Exaltation into Royal Arch Masonry which may not have been immediately apparent to you either at your own Exaltation or on any occasions on which you have witnessed the ceremony since.

It is based on a ritual known as the Perfect Ceremonies, as practised in the 19th century in Sheffield, in the Province of Yorkshire (West Riding). Certain modifications have had to be made because there were aspects of that ceremony which are no longer practised. For example, the candidate then was slipshod as a sign of humility and adoration in the same way that Moses was commanded to put off his shoes from his feet when he approached the Most High. His arms, breasts and knees were made bare as a token of sincerity and truth and he had a cable-tow round his waist in the same way as the Principal Sojourner ties a rope round his waist before descending into the vault. That was intended to symbolise the unshaken faith and constancy of the Patriarch Abraham and the preparation for sacrifice of his son Isaac, whom he bound and laid upon the altar.

Q. *How shall I know you to be a Royal Arch Mason?*

A. *By PW's and signs, but more particularly by the possession of the Sacred Name communicated to me at my Exaltation.*

Q. *Where was that Sacred Name communicated to you?*

A. *In a lawfully constituted Holy Royal Arch Chapter of Jerusalem.*

Q. *Why was your Chapter holy?*

A. *Because we bless, praise and magnify the holy name of TTALGMH, our Chapter is set in the ruins of the Holy Temple of King Solomon and we advance towards the altar whereon the Sacred Name is engraved.*

Q. *Why was your Chapter Royal?*

A. *Because several Kings participated in the labour of temple building: Solomon, King of Israel and Hiram, King of Tyre joined with Hiram the widow's son in building the first temple. Cyrus, King of Persia released the Children of Israel to return to their homeland and build the second temple and Zerubbabel, prince of the people, presided over that latter labour.*

Q. *What significance has the arch?*

A. *Beneath King Solomon's temple was a vaulted chamber containing nine arches and it was within the ninth of these that the Sacred Name was deposited.*

Q. *How were you prepared to enter the Chapter?*

A. *I was given a password and hoodwinked.*

Q. *I will thank you for that password.*

A. *Ammi Ruhamah, meaning 'My people having found mercy'.*

Q. *Why were you hoodwinked?*

A. *To represent the darkness in which the Principal Sojourner found himself on his first descent when he was unable to read the Hebrew characters on the Altar. Also to represent the darkness of the Shadow of Death in which the posterity of Adam floundered until the Most High was pleased to call them to light and immortality by the revelation of His Holy Will and Word.*

Q. *Why are four knocks given at the door of a Royal Arch Chapter?*

A. *In ancient times the number four referred to the Deity and was considered the whole number or the number of numbers or the number of perfection, representing the Divine Mind and the image of the Most High. The RA Degree being the summit and perfection of Freemasonry, the number four is the most appropriate form of introduction to this Degree and also represents the tetragrammaton, or the four letter name of God, which it is the province of the RA to disclose to those who are worthy.*

Likewise it refers to the four salutations, four words in four languages, four principal banners and four points of my Exaltation.

Q.   What are the four points of your Exaltation?

A.   Obligation, Instruction, Arch and Triangle.

Q.   Before taking your Obligation, how were you disposed of?

A.   I was received between two Sojourners and advanced towards the Sacred Shrine on which the mysteries of the RA are deposited by seven steps.

Q.   To what do these seven steps allude?

A.   To the ceremony of Passing the Veils which, although no longer practised in this country, describes the actions of Moses at the foot of Mount Horeb in the Wilderness of Sinai.

Q.   How were you raised after your Obligation?

A.   By the Principal Sojourner, at the command of the MEZ, and by five distinct movements.

Q.   Why by five distinct movements?

A.   In unison with the five points of fellowship, five signs of this Degree, five books of the Law of Moses and the tradition that the Sojourners made five distinct efforts to raise their Companions out of the vaulted chamber.

End of Part One

APPENDIX 6
The Song to the Principals

I have included this song as a personal tribute to my good friend the late Excellent Companion Sidney Benson Past Grand Standard Bearer. Sidney was an avid Royal Arch Mason with a beautiful singing voice. He lived in the Knotty Ash area of Liverpool and, being slight of stature, often likened himself to Ken Dodd's 'Diddy men'.

Sidney, however, was a native of Wigan in Lancashire, where of course there was a breakaway Grand Lodge in the 19th and early 20th centuries. This song, which Sid was always in demand to sing at Chapter installations, also came from Wigan although we don't know any more about it than that. The music is tagged on at the end, supplied not from Wigan but from the Isle of Man.

Verse 1   When Cyrus' decree the people made free
            After seventy weary years
            They struggled along without mirth or song
            As their hearts were filled with fears

For Jerusalem, so beloved of them
Lay in ruins and decay
But the three brave men, who led them then
Kept their courage up day by day.

Chorus   So here's to Joshua, one, two, three
And here's to Haggai, one, two, three
And here's to Zerubbabel, Prince of the people
Here's to the three of them, one, two, three.

Verse 2   When the Sojourners three, who were Masons free
Began to clear the ground
With a pick and crow and a shovel to throw
They delved 'til treasure they found.
Then they hi'ed away, that self same day,
To the Grand Sanhedrin old,
Who gave each one for what he'd done,
A ribbon and a jewel of gold.

Repeat Chorus

Verse 3.   Now, Royal Chapters all once a year install
Their Principals one, two and three
And we pledge them now, with a solemn vow
Our support and loyalty.
May they be famed and long acclaimed
For peace, love and loyalty
That they long may live is the toast we give
To our excellent trinity.

Repeat Chorus

Sidney died, well in his nineties, in 2011 and will be much mourned. Few of you from outside Merseyside will have heard this song and I offer it as a sincere tribute to his memory.

Epilogue

And so the story of the Royal Arch ends. We have covered the history of the Royal Arch in England and Wales, as well as in other places, and we have looked behind the symbolism of this most central of all steps on the Masonic journey. Wherever else you go in Masonry the fundamental lesson of your dependence on God and your relation with Him should never be forgotten. This you were taught in the Royal Arch and to use a modern phrase, 'You heard it here first'.

The Degree itself covers the history of the Hebrew people, the Jewish race, from the Creation to the destruction of Herod's Temple in AD 70. It is an exciting story of faith, backsliding and ultimate reconciliation with God, set against a backdrop of love, war and violence. There was a further attempt to rebuild the Temple, which members of the Order of the Red Cross of Constantine who have been installed as Knights of the Holy Sepulchre and St.John the Evangelist know about. That was by Julian the Apostate, who failed signally to achieve his purpose. As the ritual of that beautiful Degree says:

'There is no longer any Temple because the light of the Lord is universally diffused and the world has become one holy house of wisdom. The hour cometh and now is when true worshippers shall worship the Father in Spirit and truth.'

The Royal Arch Degree continues in England and Wales as it has since 1835, in a way that is unique. From time to time, changes are thought advisable – during my time in the Royal Arch in 1988 and 2004 – which are not always well received, at least not at first. But we began our sojourn by going from east to west, towards the *sanctum sanctorum*, in search of that which was lost. We failed to find it in our Third Degree and it took the destruction of the Temple by Nebuchadnezzar and the burial underground of precious treasures before we could be put in a position to rediscover them.

The Western Wall, Jerusalem.

When the Temple was finally destroyed by the Roman General (and later Emperor) Titus in AD 70 one wall was left standing 'for them to wail over' as Titus put it. It is more correctly known these days as the Western Wall but it is not a wall of the Temple, rather a retaining wall in the outer courtyard. Down the ages, Jews have

Cyprus Principals' Chapter.

prayed at that wall for the peace of Jerusalem (which has often known anything but) and in similar manner it behoves us to remember the place that brought us into the closest contact with God we have ever had in our lives, when we were exalted in the Holy Royal Arch and discovered what so many millions of people never did find – His Sacred and Mysterious Name.

'I was glad when they said unto me let us go into the House of the Lord. Our feet shall stand within thy gates, O Jerusalem. Jerusalem is builded as a city that is compact together; whither the tribes go up, the tribes of the Lord, unto the testimony of Israel, to give thanks unto the name of the Lord. For there are set thrones of judgment, the thrones of the House of David. Pray for the peace of Jerusalem, they shall prosper that love thee. Peace be within thy walls, and prosperity within thy palaces. For my brethren and companions' sakes, I will now say, peace be with you. Because of the House of the Lord our God, I will seek thy good.' [77]

I began this book by saying that it was time for a fresh look at the Royal Arch and where it sits in the Masonic 'big picture'. Hopefully reading it has helped you to find answers to that and has assisted you in your search 'for that which was lost'. In any event I thank you for taking the trouble to read it.

Duncan Moore
LARNACA, CYPRUS 2013

---

77 Psalm 122

Bibliography

The Holy Bible (King James and NIV versions)

The Complete Workings of the Royal Arch Ritual (2008)

The Aldersgate Royal Arch Ritual (Lewis Masonic 2005)

The Domatic Working of the Ceremonies of the Holy Royal Arch (Lewis Masonic 1961)

The Perfect Ceremonies of the Supreme Order of the Holy Royal Arch (H.J.Croneen 1905 and A.Lewis 1978)

The Ritual of the Holy Royal Arch as worked in the Province of Sussex (Lewis Masonic 1997)

Freemasons' Book of the Royal Arch by Bernard E. Jones (George G. Harrap 1957)

Royal Arch Working Explained by Herbert F. Inman (Spencer & Co. 1933)

Sidelights on Freemasonry (Craft and Royal Arch) by Rev. John T. Lawrence (A.Lewis 1948)

Side Lights on the Holy Royal Arch by F.G.Harmer – published privately, year unknown

The Rosslyn Hoax? by Robert Cooper (Lewis Masonic 2006)

Ezra the Scribe by Brian J. Bell (The Batham Royal Arch Lecture for 1985)

The Ritual of Royal Forest Chapter No.404 (Province of Yorkshire West Riding) published privately (1999)

Freemasons' Royal Arch Guide by E.E.Ogilvie (A.Lewis 1978)

The Origin and Development of Royal Arch Masonry by Anthony R. Ough – The Batham Royal Arch Lecture for 1991 AQC 108 (1995)

Some Observations on the Fifth Section of the Lecture in Early Royal Arch Rituals by A.J.Owen AQC 110 (1997)

The Royal Arch Jewel – An Explanation by Christopher Powell AQC 123 (2010)

Rosicrucianism and its Effect on Royal Arch Masonry by A.J. Owen AQC 123 (2010)

Promulgation and Reconciliation by C. John Mandleberg AQC 123 (2010)

Freemasonry by Alexander Piatigorsky (The Harvill Press 1997)

Fraternity Chapter No.4072 – Exaltation with Explanation by Rev Neville Barker Cryer (2002)

The Arch and the Rainbow by Rev Neville Barker Cryer (Lewis Masonic 1996)

The Freemason's Pocket Reference Book by F.L. Pick and G.N. Knight (Frederick Muller 1955)

The Royal Arch: Its Hidden Meaning by George H. Steinmetz 1946 (Macoy

Publishing and Masonic Supply Company Inc. 1979)

York Mysteries Revealed by Rev Neville Barker Cryer 2006

The History of the Wigan Grand Lodge by Eustace B. Beesley (Manchester Association for Masonic Research – private subscription)

Freemasonry in My Life by Sir James Stubbs KCVO (Lewis Masonic 1985)

The Royal Arch Journey by Rev Neville Barker Cryer 2009 (Lewis Masonic)

Royal Arch Masons and Knights Templar at Redruth, Cornwall 1791-1828 by C.J. Mandelberg and L.W. Davies 2005 (QCCC)

A Reference Book for Freemasons by Frederick Smyth (QCCC 1998)

The Freemason at Work by Harry Carr, revised by Frederick Smyth (Lewis Masonic 1992)

Jerusalem: the Biography by Simon Sebag Montefiore (Phoenix 2011)